life change for couples

A Biblical 12-Step Journey for Marriage Enrichment

A WORKBOOK

life change for couples

James M. Reeves

If you would like to have James M. Reeves come to your church or conference to do on-site training or consultation, you can contact him by email or at his website. At the time of this writing, James is able and willing to come without charge. Email: james@jamesmreeves.com; website: www.jamesmreeves.com.

Published by Kregel Publications, a division of Kregel, Inc., P.O. Box 2607, Grand Rapids, MI 49501.

For the purposes of this book, the word "alcohol" in Step One has been changed to read spouse's name. In Step Three the phrase "God as we understood Him" has been deleted. In Step Twelve the word "alcoholics" has been changed to read "others."

THE TWELVE STEPS OF ALCOHOLICS ANONYMOUS

1. We admitted we were powerless over alcohol—that our lives had become unmanageable.
2. Came to believe that a Power greater than ourselves could restore us to sanity.
3. Made a decision to turn our will and our lives over to the care of God as we understood Him.
4. Made a searching and fearless moral inventory of ourselves.
5. Admitted to God, to ourselves, and one other human being the exact nature of our wrongs.
6. Were entirely ready to have God remove all these defects of character.
7. Humbly asked Him to remove our shortcomings.
8. Made a list of all persons we had harmed, and became willing to make amends to them all.
9. Made direct amends to such people wherever possible, except when to do so would injure them or others.
10. Continued to take personal inventory and when we were wrong promptly admitted it.
11. Sought through prayer and meditation to improve our conscious contact with God as we understood Him, praying only for the knowledge of His will and the power to carry that out.
12. Having had a spiritual awakening as the result of these steps, we tried to carry this message to alcoholics, and to practice these principles in all our affairs.

Library of Congress Cataloging-in-Publication Data
Reeves, James M., 1944-
Life change for couples : a biblical 12-step journey for marriage enrichment : a workbook / James M. Reeves.
p.cm.
1. Marriage--Religious aspects—Christianity. 2. Marriage counseling—United States. 3. Communication in marriage—United States. 4. Communication in families—United States. I. Title.
BV835.R43 2012
248.8'44—dc23

2012036243

ISBN 978-0-8254-4223-0

Printed in the United States of America
13 14 15 16 17 / 5 4 3 2 1

To my wife, Laura,
my hero and life partner for over thirty years.
There is no one I would rather be in a foxhole or crisis with than her.

Contents

Foreword

The pages you are about to read can be captured in two words: *blessed wisdom*. This workbook reveals the wisdom of the Word of God as it is expressed in the principles of the Twelve Steps.

I have seen personally and professionally the miracle of God's Word come alive along with the process of healing that the Twelve Steps has offered people across the world. *Life Change for Couples* takes a couple on a unique but intelligent journey toward a better marriage.

Dr. Reeves utilizes what he has learned through decades of guiding people as they grow beyond their past. James is a practical applier of the Word of God. On page after page you will be introduced to both principles and practices.

As a Christian and a licensed psychologist, I truly enjoy what Dr. Reeves has done. He takes the hands of readers and biblically and thoughtfully directs them through each of the Twelve Steps.

I love his approach to helping marriages because it focuses on the part of the marriage spouses can change—themselves.

When people go through this time-tested process of life change, they can expect that they will be different. A different self can influence a different marriage.

Any person would benefit from reading and doing the exercises in *Life Change for Couples*. I also believe as churches embrace this material in ministry to couples, they can lay a foundation for God-purposed, healthier marriages that actually can last over the decades of life.

Great marriages not only help a couple but also their family. As one couple gets healthier and stronger, it can be the DNA of healthier marriages for generations to come, building healthy churches and communities for the future.

I encourage you to do the work in these pages and be part of the miracle God intends for your life, your marriage, and your generation.

—Douglas Weiss, PhD

Licensed Psychologist and Executive Director of Heart to Heart Counseling Center

Preface

HOW THE WORKBOOK IS DESIGNED

One of the inadequacies of many workbooks is that they are long on "filling in the blanks," but short on the explanation and illustration of important truths. The participant/reader seems to be left on his/her own to figure out the truth or to understand the depths of meaning that the principle holds. I have attempted to provide more for the reader, as the following illustrations of my workbook show.

As a Three-Legged Stool

This is neither a book simply to be read, nor is it a workbook where you just fill in the blanks. It is, in fact, a hybrid of the two. You can think of it as a three-legged stool; all three legs are important for the stability of the stool. The three legs are:

Leg One: Instruction

Each one of the steps in this process is based upon biblical principles and concepts that will be explained, illustrated, and applied, in order to make sure the participant understands the core truths upon which each chapter is based. Therefore, I have given a good portion of each chapter to that instruction and application. Some chapters have more instruction than others, depending upon the nature of the specific principle being discussed in that chapter. Instruction is necessary to make sure the participant understands what the step is about. With understanding he/she can make application.

Leg Two: Introspection

As important as the instruction and an understanding of the principles are, ultimately they are of no value for change unless the participant takes the time to do the personal introspection to see what each principle has to say to him/her. We need to ask questions such as, "How does that apply to my life right now? What change do I need in this area of my life?" What responsibility do I have according to this principle?" When instruction is joined with introspection, the stage is set for the third leg of the stool.

Leg Three: Interaction

The workbook is based upon the truth that "life change" happens best in community. I would go so far as to say that real and lasting life change happens only in the context of relationships. As we hear each other tell our stories, share insights, and confess struggles, we gain encouragement from and learn from one another. I like to say that when I am in this kind of open and honest process with you, another Christian, the Holy Spirit who is in you speaks to the Holy Spirit in me. Through you He teaches, convicts, encourages, and ultimately changes me. It is important that each person has all three legs of the stool on the ground for each step.

Another way of expressing this triad is "Teaching, Thinking, and Talking." All three are important in order to experience the full benefit of the process. When each member of the group "Suits up" (Does the work), "Shows up" (Comes to the meetings), and "Speaks up" (Shares), then the environment is created for the beginning of life change for every person in the process.

I do believe that all three legs are important. However, I have designed the workbook in such a way that if there is a person who does not have a group available to go through this process with, he or she could do it alone and receive some benefit. That would not be the optimum, but it is an option when no group is available.

As a Two-Step Dance

In Texas, we have a famous dance called the Two-Step. In fact, its full name is the "Texas Two-Step." I don't know if it originated in Texas, but we Texans at least like to think it did. So, we take credit for it, as we do with many other things.

The chapters in this workbook are like the Two-Step. Each chapter is divided into two basic parts. The first is the problem of the step. As you will see, each of the steps presents a unique and difficult challenge. I feel it best to state these challenges right up front. We know they exist for two reasons: Scripture indicates it, and experience bears it out. At the end of the day, we all have the same basic sin nature that we must do battle with. Therefore, we all have the same basic struggles and challenges. They just come at different levels. So, each chapter opens with a recognition of the challenge.

The rest of each chapter is made up of the explanation of the process. Each one of the steps has its own unique process that is required in order to work through the step. There are guidelines and instructions for each step that have been discovered over many years of practice and with the input of many people who have gone before. In other words, "This is not our first rodeo." We have been here before and have ridden this bull many times. We know him well and can help keep you from getting bucked off and stomped into the dirt, if you will listen.

As Alphabet Soup

There are twelve steps, but only ten chapters that begin with a consecutive letter of the alphabet. That is because steps 6 and 7 and steps 8 and 9 have been combined in this workbook. When we come to them you will understand why I have done that.

In each chapter there is a basic, core principle upon which that step is based. Each one of the principles is a tool. A tool for life change. When you have completed this workbook you will not be finished. You will have just begun. This workbook is designed to introduce you to these tools and teach you how to use the tools on an ongoing basis. This is just like a technical school where you learn the things you will need in order to go out and become successful in life change. As you use these tools every day of your life, you will become more effective in their use and they will become more effective in your life. In other words, these tools are being provided for you to use for the rest of your life.

For that reason, I wanted a mechanism by which anyone could learn these principles and be able to recall them at any time in sequential order. Since most of us know the first ten letters of the alphabet, I thought that would be a good structure to use.

The first step is "A"—Admitted Powerlessness. Step two is "B"—Believe the Truth, and so on, to the last step which is "J"—Just Do It! You will find this won't take much memorization skill. It will come naturally as you work through each chapter. When we come to "H," "Heed the Weeds," in chapter 8 you will see specifically how this ability to recall the steps at any time and any place will have practical application.

As a Picture Collage

Because the information in this workbook has to be easily recalled in order for it to be practical and usable, most steps have at least one visual picture to illustrate the core principle of that step. It has been proved that the mind thinks in pictures. That is why successful memory systems teach us to turn concepts and thoughts into pictures in order to be able to remember them over long periods of time. Not only that, but many of us are visual learners. I have discovered that in my own learning. If I can see something as well as hear it, I learn and retain it much more effectively. So, as you move through these steps you will be developing mental pictures that will aid your understanding and recall of the principles for application in daily life.

As a Toolbox

I carry a toolbox in the back of my truck. It is with me everywhere I go. For that toolbox to do me any good three things must happen. First, I must know how each tool works. If I don't know how the tool works it can do me no good. Second, I must have the tool with me when I need it. If it's at home in the garage when my truck breaks down it can't do me any good at all. Third, I must take the tool out and use it.

I may know how a tool works and even have it with me, but until I take it out and use it I will remain stuck by the side of the road.

The process in this book is about acquiring tools for life change. There are different tools for different purposes. I must know how each tool works, have it with me at all times, and then take it out and use it when the need arises! If even one of those three things is not accomplished, I stay stuck where I am and life change can't happen.

In *Life Change for Couples,* you will learn how each tool works and what it is for. You will be given mechanisms by which you can carry these tools with you everywhere you go. It will then be your decision whether or not you use the tool when and where it is needed to accomplish real and lasting life change.

So, there you have it. A three-legged stool, two-step dance, alphabet soup, a picture collage, and a toolbox! All the tools for Life Change? Not quite. There is one more.

As Table Talk

Historically, the dinner table has been the time when families connected. There is something about sitting around the table together with a meal, or just a cup of coffee, that is conducive to open and honest communication and sharing. During the Table Talk section, husbands' and wives' groups will meet separately. The husbands will have a male facilitator and the wives will have a female facilitator. They will do their individual work separately and their groups will meet separately. However, at the end of the main chapters I have provided a question for Table Talk. This is a time for husband and wife to share together during the week what they are discovering about themselves through this process. The focus of the time is for each individual to speak about himself or herself, not his/her spouse. It's a time for honesty, transparency, and vulnerability. This is the kind of thing we all did when we were dating, isn't it? We talked. Somehow over the years of marriage we tend to lose our ability to talk to each other. That is the beginning of separation and the drift away from each other that has brought many of us to the place we are. So, let's get around the table each week and reconnect. The facilitator will begin the session each week with the question, "How did Table Talk go this week?" This will help get the discussion started and will provide some accountability for each person to do Table Talk each week. It has been my experience in three years of field testing this material in churches all over the country that couples who do not do Table Talk do not get near as much benefit as couples who do. Without Table Talk, it is easy for this to become just another intellectual exercise where very little real life change happens. COUPLES MUST DO TABLE TALK!!!

Acknowledgments

So many people have had a part in the development of this book. I want to thank my friend, Chuck Youngman, who first took me through the Twelve Steps. His example, mentorship, and partnership in the work have been invaluable in my life and laid the foundation for this workbook.

Thanks to the brave warriors of City on a Hill and churches around the country who field tested and improved this material. They were the test pilots who took the first risks of practicing these principles. Thank you City on a Hill for being a hospital for the hurting.

Thanks to Barbara Geyer, who was part of the very first group who ever used this material with me. Barbara graciously volunteered to edit the material for me (it was pretty bad), and she became a true blessing to this process.

Thanks to my talented daughter, Tiffany, a pediatric trauma nurse practitioner, vocalist extraordinaire, wonderful mother and, as it turns out, a very talented designer and formatter. Tiffany designed the first cover for *Life Change for Couples* and was responsible for the initial layout and formatting of the entire workbook when it was first self-published. When she got her hands on it, the workbook went from plain vanilla to double chocolate almond! She's also the best daughter a father could ever have.

Thanks to my wife and life partner, Laura, who has put up with me for over thirty years. She has walked with me through every step of the process of help, hope, and healing in my life. I recognize that very much of it has been with great sacrifice on her part.

Most importantly, thank you, Lord Jesus, for being the Great Physician who is our *help*, *hope*, and *healing* and for giving us eternal truths in your Word.

Freedom Group Guidelines

TO BE REFERRED TO EACH WEEK BEFORE GROUP BEGINS

- Anonymity: We protect the identities of all group members.
- Confidentiality: Nothing that is said in the group or done in the group is ever discussed with others without permission from those involved.
- Self-Focus: We are here to work on ourselves, not on others.
- Respect for others: We do not advise, analyze, or try to "fix" others.
- Letting God work: We do not preach to others in the group but only share from our own experience, strength, and hope.
- Limited sharing: We will be considerate of the need for others to share.
- Allowance of feelings: We avoid minimizing hurts, by explaining them away, ignoring them, or avoiding them.
- Regular attendance: We agree to be here unless absolutely unable because of emergency or unavoidable circumstances.
- Listening: We will not cross-talk with another person when someone is sharing.
- Staying on the subject: We avoid discussions that do not relate to the material that we are working through that week.

- Consideration of others: We guard against offending others in the group. If someone offends us, we work it out directly with him/her.

- Taking responsibility: We will be responsible to do our work individually during the week so we have something to share in the group

APPROPRIATE SHARING

Remember: Our sharing is to be ABOUT OURSELVES, not our spouse. Behavior of our spouse is to be talked about in the group only to the extent necessary in order to discuss our own need to change or grow. Before you share something specific about your spouse, put yourself in his/her place and ask yourself, "Would I feel dishonored, betrayed, or humiliated, if he/she shared something like this with a group of people when I was not there to speak on my own behalf?" If you would not want it shared about you, then don't share it about your spouse.

It is possible to speak about behavior of your spouse in general terms and in a way that is not dishonoring to him/her and still accomplish the ultimate goal of only telling that information in order to bring the sharing back around to yourself.

For instance, if there has been marriage infidelity by your spouse, you can say that without going into graphic detail with the group. The statement of infidelity is enough to allow you to share YOUR own hurt, discuss how YOU reacted, and what YOU need to do from here.

Remember, the purpose of this group is not to give an EXPOSÉ of your spouse but to address your own issues and need for change. If both spouses are following these guidelines, then no one is dishonored and the appropriate focus is maintained.

It will be the FACILITATOR'S RESPONSIBILITY to assure that this guideline is followed.

Introduction: Welcome to the War

Welcome to the great adventure of life change! This is war. Make no mistake about it; you are about to begin perhaps the greatest adventure of your life. In the popular movie, *City Slickers*, Billy Crystal and two of his friends are searching for more to life. They realize that they need change in their lives. Every year, they get together and go away on some crazy adventure, hoping to find what they are looking for. They run with the bulls in Pamplona, Spain. They target parachute. Each year it's something new and different. One year, they head for New Mexico for a two-week cattle drive from New Mexico to Colorado. It becomes the adventure of a lifetime. In fact, it becomes a life-changing adventure. They are pushed to their limits of physical endurance. They are challenged by the elements. They're faced with a scary guy named Curly and must overcome adversity in order to bring the cattle to their destination. In the end, they finish the adventure and realize they have been changed in the process.

Your journey will have many things in common with theirs. For most of us this will be the greatest adventure of our lives. We also are on an adventure that will challenge us in new and incredible ways: a new way of thinking about God, others, and ourselves. A new way of living that can be free of the fears, habits, and behaviors that have done nothing but hinder us to this point. Along the way, there will be some challenges. You may have some people in your life who don't want you to make this journey. They will be threatened by the changes in you. You'll have to overcome that threat. You will face your own internal struggles. There will be some tall mountain peaks to climb, some deep valleys to cross, and raging rivers to navigate. To this point, your way of doing life may have brought you a lot of pain and failure, but at least it has been familiar to you! At times, you are going to want to retreat into that familiarity and run away from the new things that you are discovering. To complete the adventure you will need to face and overcome those challenges. The good news is that you don't have to face them alone.

You are going to be traveling in community. Others are with you on this journey. They are fellow adventurers and will be experiencing the same fears and challenges. You will draw encouragement from each other during the struggles along the way. You will celebrate the victories together as you stand on the precipice and see wonderful sights that you have never seen before. Freedom groups are a community of people where newcomers can experience how God has worked in the lives of others. They are a place where we can come to understand God's grace in a loving, accepting, non-judgmental environment.

There is someone else who, more than anyone, wants you to make this journey. In fact, He is going to be traveling with you. He is the loving heavenly Father. You may have never experienced Him or known Him as a loving Father, but that's exactly who He is. He wants you to know Him that way. He'll be calling to you, beckoning to you, guiding you, and cheering you on as you travel. You will be calling to Him along the way for strength and courage to face the challenges. He will give that strength and courage when you ask. Who better to have with you as a guide than One who already knows the way and wants you to find the way. He not only knows the way, He is the way. In John 14:6, Jesus said, "I am the Way, the Truth, and the Life." He wants to set you free from whatever binds you up. Jesus said in John 8:36, "So if the Son makes you free, you will be free indeed."

Finally, understand that though you must make the journey, you are not the first to do so. So many thousands have gone before you that the trail is well-worn. All you have to do is follow the path that has been laid out and you will successfully make the trip. By the way, all these who have successfully gone before . . . guess what they are doing? They are cheering you on! They are screaming at the top of their lungs, "Go for it!" "You're the man!" or "You're the woman!"

> *Therefore, since we have so great a cloud of witnesses surrounding us, let us also lay aside every encumbrance and the sin which so easily entangles us, and let us run with endurance the race that is set before us. (Hebrews 12:1)*

So how about it? Are you ready?

What are you feeling right now about the adventure? Take a few moments to write down some of the things that you are feeling now and then tell them to the heavenly Father. Just talk to Him as if to a friend because He is that and so much more.

____

____

____

In the very beginning, we want to be honest with you about an important matter. This is a Christ-centered growth and freedom group ministry. We believe that Jesus Christ is the risen Son of God and our ultimate hope is found in Him and Him alone. We feel that integrity requires we establish that fact up front. The only way to experience life and marriage to its fullest, the way God intended us to experience it, is through a faith relationship with Him through His Son, Jesus Christ. We want you to know Him intimately and have the opportunity to know that abundant life.

However, if you are not yet ready to make that commitment of your life to Him, we want you to know we are ready to accept you wherever you are in the process. We receive you as you are, and want to help you in any way we can. One of the ways that we can help you is by encouraging you to discover some eternal truths. These are truths that God has given to help you overcome some of the hindrances in your life that have brought you to this point. All truth is God's truth, and truth works. Truth always works when truth is applied. So, as you learn these truths that have their source in the Bible, God's Word, they can give you a measure of help and victory in your life. If that is all you want to receive through this freedom group process, then you can receive that. But we want you to understand there is so much more that is available to you than just help in overcoming your addiction, learning how to have healthier relationships, or help in overcoming your destructive behaviors. There is a deeper sense of peace, joy, tranquility, and power that is available to you in this life through faith in Jesus Christ. Not only that, but through faith in Him there is the promise of eternal life with Him when this earthly life ends. Through this freedom group, you will learn how to appropriate all that God has to offer you in your life through faith in Christ. It is our prayer that along the way you will accept the free gift of grace He offers you. We are praying toward that end. Please know that we understand if you have doubts and fears and struggles in coming to that point in your life. We were all at that place at one time. We are willing to support you, encourage you, and care for you, regardless of what you decide. Please know that this is a safe place for you to walk this great adventure of life change.

WHY LIFE CHANGE FOR COUPLES?

As horrible as war is, there is nothing like war to cause a nation to refocus on things that are precious and really matter. In the years leading up to World War II, America was coming out of the Great Depression. Americans were once again beginning to enjoy prosperity. The threat of Nazism was looming on the horizon, but as a nation, we resisted becoming a part of what we viewed as "Europe's problem." Even after Hitler declared war upon Great Britain, most Americans did not want to get involved. Then, on December 7, 1941, Japan attacked Pearl Harbor and in one swift move wiped out nearly the entire Pacific fleet of the United States Navy. Suddenly, Americans were reminded of what was important because everything we were as a nation was threatened. We went to war with the Axis powers to fight for our very existence.

On September 11, 2001, America was attacked again. Terrorists flew commercial airliners into the World Trade Center towers in New York City, killing thousands. Another plane flew into the very bastion of American defense, the Pentagon. A fourth went down in the fields of Pennsylvania because of the bravery demonstrated by the passengers on board. Had they not acted, that plane was most likely destined to attack the Capitol building itself. Once again, these attacks were made possible, at least in part, because Americans had come to believe this was something that could never happen on American soil. After all, these were the types of attacks that happened in Northern Ireland, or the Middle East, but certainly not the United States. That bubble of naiveté was popped, and we were forced to accept that we were in fact in a war—one against terrorism and one being fought right here on American soil.

There is another war. The question, "Why Life Change for Couples?" arises from the fact that we are involved in a war. Our Enemy doesn't fly planes or drop bombs, but do not be mistaken—he is more committed, vicious, and malicious than any human enemy could ever be. He is not physical. He is spiritual in nature and is dedicated to destroying everything good that God has created and given to those whom He created. The Bible describes him and this war in graphic language:

> *Put on the full armor of God, so that you will be able to stand firm against the schemes of the devil. For our struggle is not against flesh and blood, but against the rulers, against the powers, against the world forces of this darkness, against the spiritual forces of wickedness in the heavenly places. (Ephesians 6:11–12)*

Not only is the Enemy spiritual in nature, but he is bent upon destroying everything good God wants to do in your life, family, and marriage.

> *Be of sober spirit, be on the alert. Your adversary, the devil, prowls around like a roaring lion, seeking someone to devour. (1 Peter 5:8)*

The Bible tells us that this war began as far back as the Garden of Eden with Adam and Eve. God created them in a perfect environment and in perfect fellowship with Him, yet the Enemy sought to destroy that. He enticed them into disobeying their Creator and trusting in themselves rather than God. That was the first sin, and the result was the destruction of the perfect relationship that man and woman had with their perfect Creator. Not only that, but it brought devastation upon the first marriage relationship. Isn't it interesting that right after the fall, husband and wife immediately blamed each other for what had happened? Husbands and wives have been blaming each other ever since, to the destruction of their marriages. That is no accident. It is the result of the fall that we are always looking outside ourselves for someone else to blame.

God has provided a way back into a relationship with Him so we can know Him and experience the good in life that He desires us to have. That way is through the death, burial, and resurrection of the Son of God, Jesus Christ. God desires not only that we gain eternal life when we place our trust in Christ, but He desires to give us abundant life here on earth. The Enemy is working constantly to defeat the heavenly Father's purpose in our lives. He does that most effectively when he can destroy marriages. When he can destroy husband and wife, he can destroy children. Generation after generation, he does his work of destruction. It's past time for us to declare war. In 2009 we at City on a Hill declared war! We declared war on divorce and the destruction of marriages in our church and our community.

I had already written *Life Change for Every Christian (A biblical twelve-step process),* and we were using it in our ministry to help individuals experience emotional and spiritual growth and healing. It dawned on me one day that if every married couple would apply these biblical principles to their relationship, there would be no way the Enemy could destroy their marriages and homes. These principles would form a protection around their relationships to keep him from sowing his seeds of destruction.

So I rewrote the workbook and the result was *Life Change for Couples*. We are now in the business of storming the gates of hell. He has already declared war on us and now we have declared war back! We will no longer take a defensive stance. We are on the offensive, and we intend to take no prisoners. This really is a life or death struggle.

Welcome to the war!

1

The Healing Environment

And Jesus answered and said to them, "It is not those who are well who need a physician, but those who are sick. I have not come to call the righteous but sinners to repentance." (Luke 5:31-32)

In answer to the question of why Jesus associated Himself with people whom the religious elite of His day rejected as hopeless, Jesus referred to Himself as a "physician" who has come for those who are sick not those who are well. Of course, as you study Jesus' relationship with those same legalistic religious leaders, you come to understand His words were tongue-in-cheek. Not about His being a physician, but about the religious leaders being well. In fact, their sickness was found in their refusal to acknowledge they had any need. Jesus did in fact operate as a physician. In His earthly ministry, before the crucifixion and resurrection, He healed people physically, spiritually, and emotionally. Jesus always gravitated toward the wounded and hurting.

Without a doubt, many of the people Jesus encountered had been wounded because of their own self-will that had led them to make self-destructive choices. The story of the woman at the well, told in the fourth chapter of the Gospel of John, certainly illustrates that. She was a woman who had a pattern of getting into destructive relationships. She had been married five times and at the time was living with a man to whom she was not married. Her life had been a series of unhealthy choices, yet Jesus met her with love and compassion and a hope that life could be different. She responded to Him and found in Him a new way of doing life.

Sometimes Jesus encountered people who were wounded spiritually and emotionally by the destructive actions of others against them. Jesus' encounter with the lame and blind and deaf most often resulted in Him healing them physically. But the real healing for them was much deeper than just physical healing. In that ancient culture, someone who had a physical deformity was considered a liability and often became an outcast from society and even their own family. The emotional pain of that kind of rejection had to be much deeper than the pain of their physical infirmity. Jesus saw beyond the outer physical pain and took compassion upon the deep emotional and spiritual wounding they had received from the hands of others. No doubt, the physical healing was wonderful, but the deeper healing Jesus gave was always spiritual and emotional.

Nothing has changed over the past two thousand years. All of us who have lived on this earth have made self-destructive choices that have wounded us. We have all experienced the emotional pain of being wounded by the actions of others. Because of that, we all stand in need of healing, both emotional and spiritual. Jesus, the Great Physician, is no longer physically on this earth . . . or is He? In fact, He is. He is here on earth dwelling within all those who have trusted in Him.

> *Now you are Christ's body, and individually members of it. (1 Corinthians 12:27)*

Not only that, but the Bible says Jesus is the Head of the church. In other words, He is the brain center of the church, directing its movements and work.

> *He is before all things, and in Him all things hold together. He is also head of the body, the church. (Colossians 1:17–18a)*

The point is that Jesus, the Great Physician, has called the church, His body, to be His healing agent in the world. The Great Physician is still healing, and He wants to do His healing work through people who know Him. There is no question that there have been times when the church, the body of Christ, has not obeyed Jesus' command to be a healing community. Because the church is made up of people, and people make mistakes and have the ability to become self-willed and self-centered, sometimes the church has even been an instrument of hurt in people's lives rather than healing. What this freedom group desires to be for everyone who participates, is an instrument for God's healing touch in your life. This is a hospital where the Great Physician can do His healing work. Using the imagery of a hospital, we can draw some analogies for how this group is to function in order to be successful as His instrument of healing. Notice several things about a hospital:

EVERYONE IN A HOSPITAL HAS A NEED

Nobody goes to a hospital for a vacation! You don't go there to dine on the fine cafeteria cuisine. You don't go there to chitchat with the staff. If you check into a hospital, it is because you have realized something is wrong! You have a need!

As we have said, everyone has a need because we are all wounded by life. It's just that some people are not willing to acknowledge their need. You can be coughing up blood or staring at a baseball-size lump sticking out of your neck and still say, "I don't have a problem!" That unwillingness to acknowledge the problem doesn't change the fact that there is a problem. It just keeps you from getting the help you need!

So, you have checked in because you have recognized you have a need. Everyone in this freedom group has come to the same conclusion or you wouldn't be here! Congratulations! That means you are in a place where healing can begin.

What is the main need that has caused you to become a part of this process?

____

____

EVERYONE IN A HOSPITAL HAS AN IMPORTANT ROLE

In a hospital, you find a lot of people doing a lot of different things, but when you break down their jobs, every role is vitally important. There are the physicians who are the highly trained professionals directing the care that is given. They couldn't do their job without the hands-on caregivers who are the nurses. The nurses couldn't do their job well, and without distraction, if the orderlies didn't do their work. Then there is the janitorial staff, receptionists, cafeteria staff, administration, and so on. It takes everyone fulfilling his or her role in order for the healing work of the hospital to be accomplished.

The same is true in this hospital of the freedom group you have become a part of. Everyone in the group has an important role. Each one in the group must be open to share his or her life. When we share our need and our experience with each other, we learn that we are not alone and we gain encouragement from one another. All of us are at different places in our journey, but we are each on the same journey. Each member in the group needs to be available to encourage others as well as to be encouraged. We recognize it's a sacred trust when someone opens himself or herself up to us. We must honor that trust by taking confidentiality very seriously. That means what is shared in the group must stay within the group. That creates an atmosphere of trust that allows everyone in the group to share openly and honestly.

Beyond the confidentiality agreement, there are three things each of us must do in order to make this experience the most beneficial for ourselves and everyone involved.

1. Suit Up

This means to do the work in the workbook outside of the group. The most important part of this process will be the work that each person does during the week. This work includes Table Talk.

2. Show Up

Attend every group meeting unless you absolutely cannot be there. Every time the group is together, God is going to be speaking to us, and through us to one another. If you are not at a meeting, you will miss what God said that week. We understand that things will happen and sometimes someone may have to miss a meeting. Put in simple terms, we want this to be a priority, not a prison. Don't feel that you can never miss, but miss only when you absolutely must.

3. Speak Up

This is not a spectator sport! This is not observation, but rather participation. When there is a member who never shares, it can create fear and suspicion in other members, and that will hinder their sense of freedom to share.

So, if you suit up, show up, and speak up, you will give and receive the maximum benefit from the group process.

If you are willing to accept your role of giving and receiving encouragement and the commitment to confidentiality, will you sign your name?

EVERYONE IN A HOSPITAL CAN FEEL SAFE

If everybody is admitting their need to be there, and everyone is pitching in to do their part for the healing work of the hospital to be accomplished, then every person in the hospital can feel safe! We want you to know that this group is a safe place for healing to take place!

A hospital is a place where you can and should drop your guard. In fact, when you check into a hospital, they issue you a garment that illustrates that truth. The dreaded hospital gown. The hospital gown wasn't designed for concealment! It was designed for easy access! Often in the first couple of days someone is in the hospital and wearing that gown, they are very careful to make sure the back is overlapped and tied very tightly. But, after awhile, that no longer seems as important and they just start walking down the hall with the back flapping, and they don't care anymore! By that time, they have decided they don't really need to hide anymore, because everyone is wearing the same thing and the emphasis is on healing, not looking! Besides, they have been poked and prodded in every imaginable place.

What freedom and release there is in dropping the guard and, in a safe environment, becoming completely transparent! No mask! No pretense. No need to impress. Just openness, honesty, support, and the beginning of being set free from things that have caused nothing but pain and bondage. We want to welcome you to that safe place.

What are some feelings that you are experiencing right now after you have read this? How does it make you feel to think about being completely honest in this group?

____

____

____

____

THE GOAL OF THE PROCESS

Every adventure has a starting place and a chosen destination or end result. This adventure is no different. The starting place is wherever you are right now. What is the destination? Where do we want to finally be at the end of this great adventure? In other words, "What will success look like?" Put in the context of the hospital metaphor we have already used, when someone checks into this hospital, what is the prescription for healing? What are the things we want to see achieved so that healing can take place? I want to use three words that express the prescription for healing and give a picture of the goal of this process. The first word is . . .

Integrity

Integrity is an important word with many applications and definitions. For this process, integrity relates to how consistent the internal life is with the external.

> **Integrity: When what is presented on the outside is the same as what is actually on the inside.**

We are living with integrity when our outside persona is the same as our inside person. Integrity is God's goal in our lives. In fact, integrity is woven into the very fabric of creation.

When my kids were still at home, we frequently spent Christmas at Disney World. On our way to the park, we were in a great hurry to get there, so we traveled the interstate all the way. But leaving was a sad time, so we always took a back way out that had us driving through the citrus orchards for the first couple of hours. We had a favorite orchard where we always stopped. It was one of those "pick your own fruit" orchards where you get a sack and go out and pick what you want right off the tree. There were rows of orange trees, grapefruit trees, tangerines, and so on. Guess what? I never picked an orange and peeled it only to find an apple inside! Why? Because God's creation has integrity. What is advertised on the outside is what is actually on the inside!

That principle applies to all of God's creation until it comes to people, doesn't it? All of a sudden, a part of God's creation doesn't have integrity. We often live lives on the outside that aren't anything like what we really feel on the inside. It wasn't always that way though. The Bible tells us that the trouble began in the Garden of Eden when Adam and Eve sinned against God.

> *Then the eyes of both of them were opened, and they knew that they were naked; and they sewed fig leaves together and made themselves loin coverings. (Genesis 3:7)*

Before sin entered their lives, they were fine with their nakedness! But suddenly, when they had sinned, they felt the compulsion to cover up! People have been covering up ever since. Adam and Eve covered up with fig leaves. We use all kinds of things to cover up with. We use education. Get lots of it and make it look like you have it all together because you have so much knowledge. We use money. Wear fine things, drive fine cars, live in fine houses, and have lots of investments, so we will look good on the outside. We use success. Become successful or important so others believe everything is great in our lives. We use religion. It's true! Some people actually hide behind religion! Do all the outward things like go to church, read the Bible, pray, and use religious language so people will think everything is okay on the inside. Jesus, in fact, attacked a group of people called the Pharisees for that very thing. They were outwardly very religious, but Jesus had a pretty straightforward message for them:

> *"Woe to you, scribes and Pharisees, hypocrites! For you are like whitewashed tombs which on the outside appear beautiful, but inside they are full of dead men's bones and all uncleanness. So you, too, outwardly appear righteous to men, but inwardly you are full of hypocrisy and lawlessness." (Matthew 23:27–28)*

When all is said and done, integrity isn't something we do (outside); it's something we are (inside). Before the Great Physician can do His work of healing in our lives, we have to move into integrity! So, what is the pathway to integrity?

There is a paradox here. The road to integrity, and thus the road to healing, is a road we avoid with everything that is in us. We search high and low for another way to get to completeness. There is only one road and it is the one we fight every step of the way. The road is brokenness. Brokenness is when we come to the end of ourselves. It's only at the end of ourselves that we find the beginning of God. When we come to the beginning of God, we come to the beginning of hope. Brokenness is simply that place where we give it all up! We recognize that we are at the end of ourselves.

Everything in our culture speaks about moving up! Climb the ladder of success. See you at the top! We are upwardly mobile! Here is the great paradox.

Paradox: The road to integrity is a descending road. It is not a place you climb up to. It is a place you crawl down to.

Brokenness is that place where we give it all up. Where we come to the end of ourselves. What a wonderful place to be, because it is only in that place that God actually becomes our healer. Until that time, He is really in opposition to us. That may sound strange, but that is exactly what the Bible says.

But He gives a greater grace. Therefore it says, "God is opposed to the proud, but gives grace to the humble." (James 4:6)

As long as we act in our pride and arrogance, covering up the truth about ourselves, God is in opposition to us! But the moment we come to the end of ourselves and drop our pretenses, He is there to give grace. Jesus called it becoming "poor in spirit." He said in Matthew 5:3, "Blessed are the poor in spirit, for theirs is the kingdom of heaven." Listen to that! Jesus effectively says, "I'll give you everything that is available in my kingdom, if you will just come to the end of yourself!"

The next step is confession. The Bible tells us confession is supposed to go in two directions. It must first go toward God.

If we say that we have no sin, we are deceiving ourselves and the truth is not in us. If we confess our sins, He is faithful and righteous to forgive us our sins and to cleanse us from all unrighteousness. (1 John 1:8–9)

The word translated as "confess" in the New Testament (which was originally written in Greek) is the Greek word *homologeo*, which means literally, "to speak the same as." So, when we confess to God, we are coming into agreement with what He already knows! We aren't telling Him anything He doesn't already know. He is just waiting for us to agree with Him. Then, we must confess to each other.

Therefore, confess your sins to one another, and pray for one another so that you may be healed. (James 5:16)

Real integrity requires that we be willing to confess in both directions. We confess to God and to one another. We confess to God to experience spiritual healing. We confess to one another to promote emotional and relational healing.

Confession is the equivalent of taking that hospital gown and untying the back of it! It's letting it flap in the breeze! Guess what? When we do that, we discover that not only did God already know what was beneath it but most of the people around us already knew as well! If we are really insecure and we confess our insecurity, we discover that most people who know us already knew that about us! They aren't really shocked by it! It's then we can begin to live with integrity.

Principle: The main hindrance to integrity is fear. I cannot live with integrity as long as I need your approval or fear your disapproval.

As long as I need approval to validate my worth and value, or I fear the way disapproval will cause me to feel about myself, I will continue to live without authenticity. That need will drive me to wear a mask and present the persona I believe will gain approval, or at least not solicit disapproval. When I can live without that fear, I am free to live with integrity.

How much of your life is driven by the need for approval or fear of disapproval?

____

____

____

____

Begin right now to think of some things you are hiding. What is different on your outside from what is really on your inside?

____

____

____

____

____

Perseverance

It doesn't do any good to check into a hospital and then leave before the healing has taken place. If we only begin a journey, but don't finish it, then we haven't accomplished very much have we? We have to be willing and able to go the distance. When someone comes to the place of integrity through brokenness and confession, they have begun the process of growth and healing. But they have only begun. To get all that is available to us, we have to go the whole way.

Most people can act differently, feel differently, and even think differently for a short time. A few moments or a few days. But real change doesn't happen in a few moments or even a few days. It takes time for real change to take place. Real and lasting change comes only through a new way of thinking. All our actions are based upon systems of thinking. So, it stands to reason that for God to bring real change in our lives, He must change the way we think. That takes time.

> *Therefore I urge you, brethren, by the mercies of God, to present your bodies a living and holy sacrifice, acceptable to God, which is your spiritual service of worship. And do not be conformed to this world, but be transformed by the renewing of your mind, so that you may prove what the will of God is, that which is good and acceptable and perfect. (Romans 12:1–2)*

The point is, real change is a process that happens over time. To get the benefit of that process, we must persevere through the entire process. Don't give up! Go the distance through the valleys and the mountaintops, the ups and downs of growth!

Throughout your journey, this group wants to provide three tools to help you complete the process. You will receive these "helps" from others and will be called upon at times to give them to others in the group.

1. Hope

When people lose hope, they give up. We have to believe that real and lasting change is, in fact, possible in order for us to go the distance. One of our sources of hope is from seeing real change in others and hearing their stories of transformation. Along the journey, don't be bashful about sharing the progress you are making in any area of your life. There may be someone in the group that week who is just about to give up. Hearing the results that you are experiencing can give them the hope they need to continue on. The next week, it may be you who needs the hope to continue.

2. Healing

This journey will be difficult at times. We will be facing issues and confronting the need for change and, at times, it can be very frightening. At those times, we will need to be aware of the good things that have already happened along the way. Remembering that can give us the courage to face the next challenge. Don't hesitate to encourage others in the group when you see even the smallest amount of progress in their lives. Something like, "Hey, that third eye sticking out of your forehead isn't gone but it isn't as noticeable as it used to be!" You get the idea. Encouragement gives us the courage to continue. Remember, God doesn't expect perfection, just progress. When you see progress in someone's life, even if it is very small progress, encourage him or her.

3. Help

For each one of us to go the distance, we will need help. All of us need help. The key is to have relationships of loving accountability. God could just zap each one of us and instantly heal us of all our struggles and foibles. He is certainly capable of doing that and in some instances He may choose to bring healing in that kind of way. But the normal process by which He brings growth and healing seems to be in the context of relationships. He does His normal work of healing through people! Understand that as you travel on this journey you need the others who are traveling and they also need you. As you allow yourself to open up to them and allow them to open up to you, the greatest healing becomes possible.

In general, do you consider yourself to be a finisher?

____

Explain:

____

____

____

____

How can the people in this group help you to be a finisher? To go the distance through the freedom group process?

____

____

____

Wholeness

Wholeness is the ultimate and final goal of the process. Wholeness is what the process is all about! It's why we traverse the difficult and challenging terrain. It's why we persevere when the going isn't easy. We all need and want to be "whole."

Wholeness: When you come to the point of emotional and spiritual health where you can give more than you have to take.

Have you ever been around someone who takes all the time? They take and take and eventually they suck the life out of everyone around them. That's okay for someone who is just beginning the process of growth. For a period of time, we sometimes need to receive more than we can give. But there has to come a time when each of us crosses the line where we can begin to give more than we need to take. That is the place called wholeness.

We live in a world that says "It's all about me!" Wholeness is when we wake up and realize, "Hey! It isn't all about me!" Wholeness is when I'm willing to say, "I have received so much that now I must begin to give."

Principle: The key that ultimately unlocks the door to wholeness is gratitude.

The catalyst that moves us from being fragmented into wholeness is gratitude. Without a deep sense of gratitude for what we have been given, we spend our entire lives taking. Life continues to be "all about me." The deeper the sense of gratitude, the more we move toward wholeness.

In Luke 17, we are told the story of ten leprous men Jesus healed. Understand that in Jesus' day, leprosy was the worst thing that could happen to someone. Not only because leprosy caused fingers, toes, ears, and other body parts to rot off until the person ultimately died, but even worse than that, lepers were social outcasts and completely segregated from society. They could only associate with other lepers as they watched each other die. Jesus came across a group of ten of them one day and had compassion on them and healed them all. Nine of them went their way. Only one came back and fell on his face at Jesus' feet to give Him thanks. Jesus asked the piercing question, "Weren't there ten who were healed? Where are the other nine?"

The goal of this process is to move every single one of us into the place of the one who came back to—the place of gratitude. Where do you think you will be at the end of this journey? Do you know how you will be able to know? When the journey is complete, will you be willing to begin the journey again and again and again? Still receiving more growth each time you travel, but each time able and willing to give away more than you receive? In other words, your own needs have brought you to the journey this time for yourself. Will you be willing to take the journey again in the future, not only for yourself, but also for others? Perhaps you will lead others in this process in the future.

If, at the end of this journey, your heart is so filled with gratitude to God for the growth and healing you have received, the only logical response you can give is to give that away to others. That is wholeness. That is success. That is life change.

May God bless you as you move forward in the process of life change.

List some things you have to be grateful to God for in your marriage.

1. ______________________________

2. ______________________________

3. ______________________________

4. ______________________________

5. ______________________________

What do you intend to do as a result of this chapter?

____

____

____

____

TABLE TALK

What is the most important thing about you that relates to this chapter that you will share with your spouse this week?

____

____

____

____

2

The Emotional/Spiritual Principle[1]

One of the most devastating influences in any human relationship, especially marriage, is a failure to understand and respect this principle. As we will see, it is also devastating in our relationship with God. When the truth of this principle is embraced, accepted, and acted upon, relationships grow in depth and intimacy. That's a good thing. However, when it is ignored, relationships stagnate or deteriorate. I have developed this principle fully in both of my previous books, *Refuge*, and *Life Change for Every Christian,* but because it is so important, and because some may not have been exposed to those resources, I will revisit the principle here.

> **Principle: Your spiritual maturity will never go beyond your emotional maturity.**

This can be restated in a number of ways:

- Your spiritual growth will never go beyond your emotional growth.
- You can never have a more intimate relationship with God than you are capable of having with other people.
- Your level of emotional maturity will always create a ceiling for your spiritual maturity.
- If you desire to grow deeper in an intimate relationship to the heavenly

1. Used by permission of Kregel Publications. Originally appeared in *Refuge* by James M. Reeves.

Father, you must grow in your capacity to have deeper intimate, soul-to-soul relationships with others.

That's because God has created us both as emotional and spiritual beings and the two are inseparably linked. I have seen this connection many times in people's lives. When they begin to deal with emotional wounds and the things that result from those wounds, not only do their human relationships grow in depth, but their spiritual relationship also deepens. Why does this happen? Because the emotional ceiling is raised. The hindrance to spiritual maturity is being removed.

We have at times been guilty of leading people to believe that the answer to all their problems, whether spiritual or relational, lies completely in the disciplines of the Christian life. Just pray more, study more, give more, serve more. Just love Jesus more and it's all going to get better. So people set out on a life of trying to grow by doing those things, only to end up in frustration and stagnation. As important as the disciplines of the Christian life are, they will be ineffective if there are emotional barriers that have not been dealt with and healed. This process is about addressing those emotional issues and beginning to remove those barriers so that relational as well as spiritual growth can happen. This is because they are intricately linked in Scripture.

DEFINE SOME TERMS

Before we can get into the nuts and bolts of this discussion, we first have to define some terms. What is spiritual maturity and what is emotional maturity?

Spiritual Maturity

Some who have been in church for many years often have difficulty with this principle and the difficulty comes at the point of their definition of spiritual maturity. So let's begin with a question. How would you define spiritual maturity?

____

____

____

____

It's quite possible you defined spiritual maturity based upon the Christian disciplines—going to church regularly, praying, reading and studying the Bible. While all of these qualities are good and certainly important, they are not the true measure of spiritual maturity. In fact, the Pharisees, with whom Jesus was constantly embroiled in controversy, did many of those activities to the extreme. Still, Jesus told them they had no connection to the heavenly Father at all! Their hearts were far from God.

> *You hypocrites, rightly did Isaiah prophesy of you: "This people honors Me with their lips, but their heart is far away from Me. But in vain do they worship Me, teaching as doctrines the precepts of men." (Matthew 15:7–9)*

In essence, Jesus is saying, "You think you are the spiritual elite. You think you are spiritually mature because you do all these things but you are spiritually shallow because your hearts are far from God." So we need to have a new definition of spiritual maturity.

> **Spiritual Maturity: An increasing capacity to have an intimate relationship with the heavenly Father.**

God created us for a relationship with Him. God is Spirit so this relationship is a spiritual relationship. Therefore, spiritual maturity is reflected in an increasing capacity for an intimate spiritual relationship with Him.

Emotional Maturity

Let's begin this with a diagnostic question as well. How would you define emotional maturity?

____

____

____

____

If spiritual maturity is about our capacity for intimacy with God, emotional maturity is about our capacity for intimate relationships with people! God also created us for relationships with each other. As we grow in that capacity, we are growing in emotional maturity.

> **Emotional Maturity: An increasing capacity to experience and maintain lasting intimate relationships with other people.**

The truth is that emotionally immature people have little capacity for developing and maintaining lasting, intimate relationships with others. Why? This will be addressed in a moment, but let me just state it for now. Emotional immaturity results from emotional woundedness. Emotional woundedness creates emotional/spiritual issues that prevent intimate relationships. The principle states that these two types of maturity are connected according to the plan of God. Therefore, the spiritual cannot be greater than the emotional! You cannot be more intimate with God (spiritual maturity) than you are capable of being with people (emotional maturity)!

I know some of you are arguing with me in your mind right now. At first this is difficult to understand or accept because it is so contrary to what most of us have been taught. It is important we understand if this connection is really of God.

IS THERE A BIBLICAL BASIS FOR THIS CONNECTION?

There better be, because if there isn't, then it's just the word of man, not the Word of God. All that matters is the Word of God. In truth, the Scripture does reveal that in God's divine order, spiritual maturity (how you relate to God) and emotional maturity (how you relate to others) are intricately linked. To grow spiritually we must address the emotional blocks. That is the essence of the emotional/spiritual principle.

Liar, Liar, Liar!

> *Beloved, let us love one another, for love is from God; and everyone who loves is born of God and knows God. The one who does not love does not know God, for God is love . . . If someone says, "I love God," and hates his brother, he is a liar; for the one who does not love his brother whom he has seen, cannot love God whom he has not seen. (1 John 4:7–8, 20)*

That's a fairly straightforward connection. God measures our ability to love Him, whom we cannot see, by our ability, or willingness, to love others whom we can see. It is a contradiction to say we love Him when we don't love others! The vertical is limited by the horizontal.

Stop the Worship Service!

> *"Therefore if you are presenting your offering at the altar and there remember that your brother has something against you, leave your offering there before the altar and go; first be reconciled to your brother, and then come and present your offering." (Matthew 5:23–24)*

Jesus indicates that our worship, our vertical relationship, is hindered by broken relationships on the horizontal level. Stop the music, climb over chairs if you have to, but go and get right. Then come back and present your offering to God! The broken horizontal relationship will become a block to the vertical relationship.

Limit My Forgiveness, Lord!

> *"And forgive us our debts as we also have forgiven our debtors." (Matthew 6:12)*

You recognize that verse. It's part of the model prayer, commonly called the Lord's Prayer. When you look at it closely, you will recognize that this is a request on our part for God to limit our experience of His forgiveness to the level we have given forgiveness to others! We pray, forgive us "as" we have forgiven others. If I am refusing to forgive, then I am asking God to limit my experience of His forgiveness to that level. Jesus taught us to pray this way! And the actual truth is, "You can never experience or live in the fullness of the forgiveness you have received in Christ, until you are willing to forgive others the way He has forgiven you." Again, the vertical and horizontal connect.

Spiritual Babies

> *And I, brethren, could not speak to you as to spiritual men, but as to men of flesh, as to infants in Christ. I gave you milk to drink, not solid food; for you were not yet able to receive it. Indeed even now you are not yet able, for you are still fleshly. For since there is jealousy and strife among you, are you not fleshly, and are you not walking like mere men? (1 Corinthians 3:1–3)*

This is perhaps one of the clearest examples of this "linkage" in the New Testament. The Corinthian Christians were immature. However, it wasn't because they hadn't been Christians very long. In fact, they had been. They were still spiritually immature because of their immaturity in how they related to one another. The apostle Paul says, "Are you not still fleshly?" The flesh in Scripture is the opposite and opposing force of the Spirit. You can't live in the "flesh" and live in the "Spirit" at the same time. So their emotional immaturity (jealously, strife) was both the evidence of spiritual immaturity and the cause of it!

Husbands, Watch Out!

At one point in Scripture, husbands are warned that how they relate to their wives can even have a detrimental effect on their prayer life! Ouch! That should be a wake-up call to all husbands.

You husbands in the same way, live with your wives in an understanding way, as with someone weaker, since she is a woman; and show her honor as a fellow heir of the grace of life so that your prayers will not be hindered. (1 Peter 3:7)

This passage brings up several questions, but one central truth cannot be ignored. Whatever it means to do this, husbands had better live with their wives in an understanding way and grant them honor as fellow heirs of the grace of life, or it is going to cause a problem in their open communication with the Father! God's ear to a husband's prayer is affected by the honor that he gives his wife! Heads up, husbands.

There are many other teachings within Scripture that confirm the emotional/spiritual principle, but hopefully this is enough to help the reader begin to grasp its reality. Now, as you read Scripture, keep your ears tuned to this connection and you will see it often.

We cannot divorce how we relate to one another from how we relate to God. He certainly doesn't separate the two. Therefore, anything in me that hinders my relationships with others will hinder my relationship to the Father.

THE CORE OF THE CONNECTION

The core of this connection is found in what the Bible calls the things that are the result of emotional woundedness and thus emotional immaturity. Issues such as unforgiveness, anger, and bitterness the Bible calls "sin." Sin has a devastating effect upon the Holy Spirit in the believer. Later, I will develop that thought further. For now, let me say it isn't enough for us to just tell people they need to deal with these issues. People need a place and a process where they can accomplish it! This group is the place and now you are involved in the process.

One bad apple spoils the whole bunch. Often, people believe they can harbor bitterness or resentment or unforgiveness toward just one person and it won't affect any other relationship. That simply isn't true. The truth is, all of these negative responses do more than just defile that single relationship. They have a much more far-reaching effect according to the Scripture.

Pursue peace with all men, and the sanctification without which no one will see the Lord. See to it that no one comes short of the grace of God; that no root of bitterness springing up causes trouble, and by it many be defiled. (Hebrews 12:14–15)

The problem with bitterness, anger, unforgiveness, and the like, is that they don't defile just a relationship. They defile me! I become defiled by the bitterness I hold on to. It becomes like the poison from a ruptured appendix that spreads throughout the entire body. Therefore, if I am defiled by bitterness, then every relationship in my life is going to be touched by it. It can't be compartmentalized. If you are harboring anger, bitterness, or unforgiveness toward one person, it doesn't stay there. It affects your relationship to your spouse, your children, your work associates, everything. Why? Because wherever you go, there you are! If you are defiled, then every relationship is infected. Not only your human relationships, but your relationship to God as well.

Are you getting this? Try it sometime. Put a spoiled apple in a basket with fresh apples and see how long it takes before the whole bunch is rotten. Poison spreads. Rottenness spreads and ruins everything it touches.

THE SOURCE OF EMOTIONAL IMMATURITY

I don't want to be redundant but let me spell it out clearly. I have addressed the source of emotional immaturity already but let me state it clearly again before we move on. Emotional immaturity is the result of emotional woundedness. We are wounded emotionally by the things people say to us, do to us, and take from us. Often these wounds begin in childhood when we are the most vulnerable. However, they can happen anytime in life.

If the wound is not healed (the purpose of this process) then things such as anger, bitterness, resentment, fear, insecurity, and unforgiveness can be birthed in us. Those are relationship killers! Not only the relationship with the person who wounded us, but in every possible relationship!

When emotional healing begins to happen, we begin to release anger, bitterness, and unforgiveness. Two very positive things begin to happen. First, we raise the ceiling on our capacity to have intimate human relationships. The blocks are being removed. The poison is being destroyed by the antibiotic of emotional healing. Our ability to relate to our spouse in emotional intimacy increases. Our ability to relate to everyone in our lives goes to a new and deeper level. At the same time, the ceiling is raised on our ability to move into deeper intimacy with the Father.

Christians who have stagnated in their relationship with God, even though they have continued doing all of the activities they have always done, such as church attendance, Bible study and prayer, find renewed spiritual growth when they begin to experience the healing of emotional wounds. For the first time in their lives those activities are able to accomplish their purpose. They move from being just religious activities, to pathways into the presence of the living God. Not only that, but they find deeper joy in human relationships because they are able to relate at a more intimate level.

This relationship can be illustrated by what I call the Emotional/Spiritual Ladder. All of us are at some point on the ladder of emotional/spiritual maturity, depending upon our emotional woundedness and desire for spiritual maturity. The ladder assumes that a person desires spiritual maturity but is stagnated. If that is true, then when emotional issues are addressed, and emotional wounds are healed, a person will move up the ladder toward greater emotional maturity. As that happens, spiritual maturity is able to move to higher levels as well. Why? Because the emotional barriers are being removed.

EMOTIONAL/SPIRITUAL LADDER

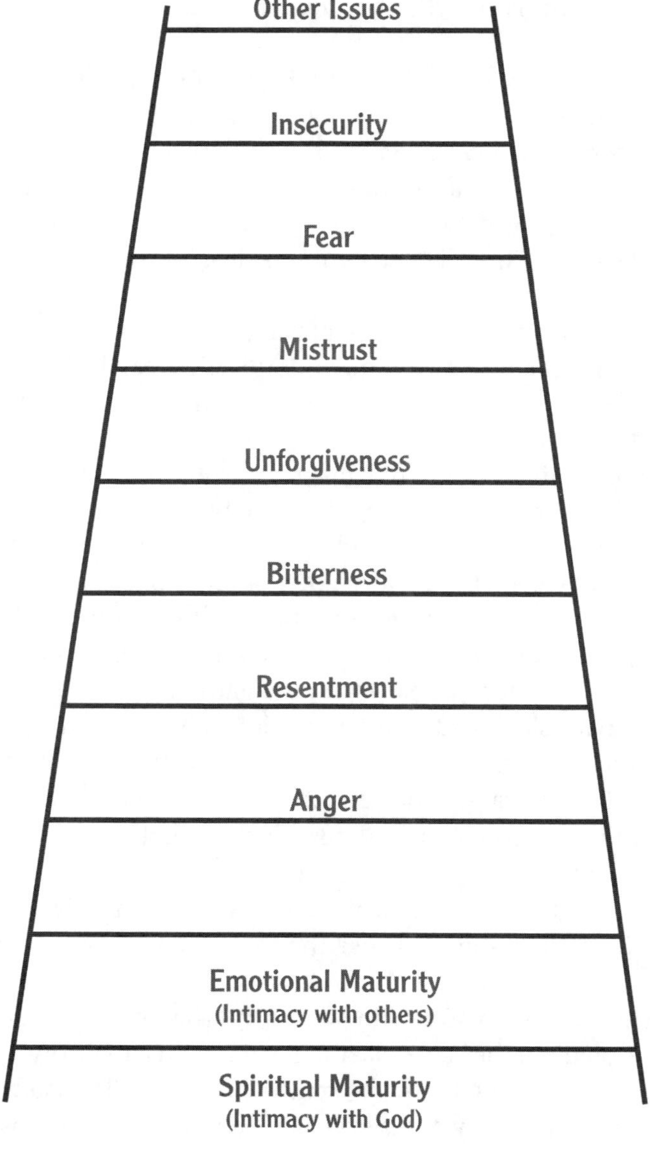

Another way the relationship can be illustrated is with the Emotional/Spiritual Circle.

We must begin at the top of the circle with grace, then proceed to faith, peace, love, fellowship, and ultimately worship. At each point around the circle, we are moving one step at a time toward emotional maturity, and thus spiritual maturity, which is expressed as worship.

Worship, simply defined, is an expression of love to God. The goal of all worship is to have unhindered freedom of an expression of love and intimacy with God. That is, at its essence, spiritual maturity.

EMOTIONAL/SPIRITUAL CIRCLE

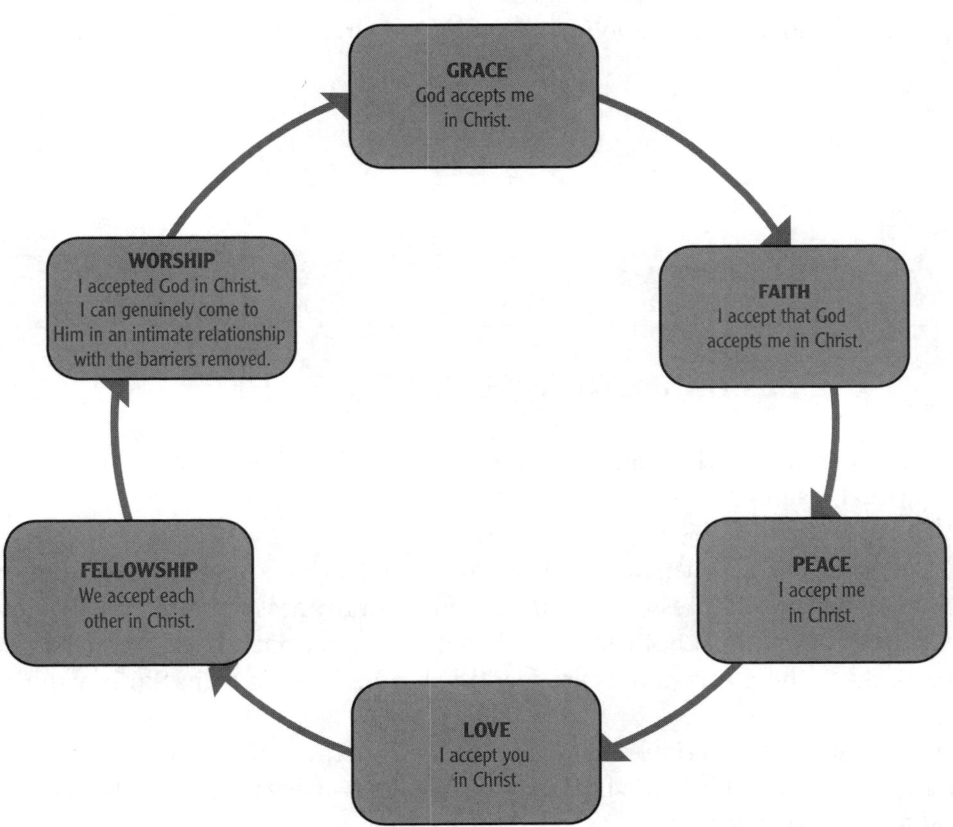

The answer to the question, "Why a life change process?" is because we all need healing at one level or another. We have all been wounded by the fall and sin, both ours and others' against us. None have escaped unscathed. If we are going to continue to grow in our spiritual, relational and married life, then we must grow in our emotional life. The two cannot be separated.

How willing are you to look into yourself and see what emotional wounds may be causing problems in your marriage?

____

____

____

____

What are some areas of emotional healing you already know are needed?

____

____

____

____

CONNECTING THE DOTS FURTHER

Truth: Our wounds have an emotional source but have both an emotional and spiritual result.

As I have stated, when we are hurt by others, those are emotional hurts and things like anger, bitterness, resentment, and unforgiveness are often created in us. The source is emotional but the result is not only emotional. It is spiritual as well. Why? Because these very things are identified in Scripture as sin. Sin is a spiritual problem.

In Romans 7, the Scripture develops the truth of the battle we fight between the spirit and the flesh. This battle has been pictured as two dogs in a fight. Which dog is going to win? The one that has been fed the most.

The point is, what determines which one wins in our lives, the flesh or the spirit, is which one we are feeding the most. We need to feed the Spirit dog and starve the Flesh dog.

Now we can begin to connect the dots of the emotional/spiritual connection further. What is the effect of sin in the Christian's life? The indwelling Holy Spirit is "grieved," as Ephesians 4:30 says, and is "quenched," as I Thessalonians 5:19 says. Since God is

Spirit, and it is by means of the indwelling Holy Spirit we have communion with Him, if the Spirit is "grieved" and "quenched" by sin, then our ability to experience intimacy with Him is hindered! Therefore, when we deal with the results of our emotional wounds, we release forgiveness, bitterness, and anger, and we are clearing the blocks to intimacy with others and with God. The Spirit is no longer "grieved" and "quenched." He is free to move us into deeper intimacy with our spiritual heavenly Father. The blocks to intimacy with the Father are removed and the way is opened wide.

What are some ways you have been emotionally wounded?

____

____

____

____

____

What have been some of the relational results you have seen in your marriage?

____

____

____

____

____

What is the most important thing you have learned in this chapter?

____

____

____

____

TABLE TALK

What is the most important thing about you that relates to this chapter that you are going to share with your spouse this week?

JOURNAL

3

The Pile Principle

The summer of 2005, my son was scheduled to play in a golf tournament in Myrtle Beach, South Carolina. He flew so he wouldn't have to play competitive golf after a twenty-hour drive in the car, but I jumped in my car with my son's golf bag to drive from my home near Fort Worth, Texas, to his tournament. I timed my trip to arrive in Myrtle Beach about the same time my son's plane landed.

As I barreled down Interstate 20 that day, I spotted, strangely enough, a big, stinking heap of garbage by the side of the road. It all zipped by in a flash, but it looked rotting and revolting and the sight prompted a variety of thoughts to surface in my mind. I had been mulling these ideas over for years in a sort of jumbled-up form, but something about seeing that pile of garbage made these truths come together. I pulled out a notebook from behind my car seat and began to scribble down thoughts as they came, while steering with my leg. I suppose I should have pulled over, but the thoughts were flying at me so fast I was afraid I'd lose inspiration if I stopped. Thank goodness for cruise control.

What formed in my mind that day was something I named in honor of that big pile of roadside garbage. I call it the "Pile Principle."[1] It's a fairly straightforward principle.

Principle: The pile of emotional garbage we carry throughout our lives is what sabotages our lives and relationships with God and others.

People sometimes use the term "emotional baggage" to describe much of what I'm talking about with the Pile Principle. But in my mind, the imagery of helping people open their bags and empty them out has always left something to be desired. A suitcase seems too nice, too sanitary, too folded and pressed. Conversely, garbage is

1. Used by permission of Kregel Publications. Originally appeared in *Refuge* by James M. Reeves.

repulsive, smelly, and putrid. Nothing you want hanging around your house for any length of time. A big pile of garbage is all slimed up with eggshells and cold coffee grounds and the moldy casserole that you found lurking in the back of your fridge. You're pressed to get rid of it as quickly and as thoroughly as possible.

In addition to new core imagery, what made the Pile Principle work for me in describing emotional baggage were five truths that progressed logically and sequentially from the extended metaphor. That's what I was working so hard to write down that day in the car as the truths unfolded quickly in my mind. In the Hospital Church, we have found these truths extremely helpful in bringing people to an understanding of their need to deal with emotional wounds in their life. The Pile Principle has also been very useful for many in understanding why they do destructive things or why their relationships and marriage never seem to work very well.

FIVE TRUTHS

Truth 1: Everybody Has a Pile

Our piles of emotional garbage come in all sizes and shapes, and from all kinds of sources, but one thing is certain, we all have a pile. None of us walk through this fallen world without collecting some amount of emotional garbage. We are fallen people who live in a fallen world with other fallen creatures. We have all been wounded. And we all have the capacity to wound others.

With each wound we receive (or give), our pile of emotional garbage grows a little or a lot, depending on the wound. The acceptance of this truth is the first step toward healing. It's also the most difficult one for most of us to wrap ourselves around. It's much easier to convince ourselves that we're exempt from the pile.

Denial comes in all shapes and sizes but always has one thing in common: it's not a river in Egypt. We must overcome it. We must see the reality of our woundedness in order to get through it and gain victory over it. If we don't, we will stay stuck where we are.

In a general sense, these emotional wounds come from three sources:

Things People Say to Us

"Sticks and stones may break my bones but words will never hurt me" might sound good on the playground but it simply isn't true. If it were true, most of us would be in much better shape. Few of us have received any lasting wounds from sticks and stones, but most of us have been wounded by words. The impact of words in our lives can be seen from the earliest days on the playground, when other children hurled hurtful epithets at us, such as fatty, ugly, stupid, and the like. Or perhaps a teacher spoke negatively about a child's ability to learn and that created a wound. The tongue's negative impact can often be reinforced in hurtful and degrading things parents sometimes say to children. These words become recordings we play back all the way into adulthood. They can direct our lives and destroy our lives if they are never confronted and countered with truth.

For instance, for most of my life, I have had a tape that has turned itself on at times that is titled, "Poor white trash." It has been a relentless voice for most of my life in describing how I see myself. Even now, if I am not careful it will begin to play. Most of the things I have accomplished in my life have been done within the context of a struggle to drown out its screech. I grew up believing I was poor white trash, then it was reinforced by the words and attitudes of others.

A close friend from college and seminary days is an example of the other end of the social spectrum. Unlike me, he was always "the good kid." He always got high grades and kept his nose clean; he was a leader in his church youth group and was a kid other parents encouraged their kids to emulate. His father was a successful and wealthy businessman, and my friend felt the expectation—and pressure—of reaching a similar level of success with his career. After high school, he went on to college to study for the ministry. After college, he received two graduate degrees from seminary. Today he is a pastor. While we were in seminary, he began to seek help for the emotional wounds he had received from the tongue of his perfectionistic, controlling father. He began suffering from depression and admitted to having difficulty in relationships. During that time, one day between seminary classes he said to me, "James, do you know what my dad did to me one time? When I was sixteen years old he waited until I was completely naked, sitting in the bathtub, and he walked in and said to me, 'Son, you don't really like me and I don't really like you. But until you leave home, here's how it's going to be.'" The father proceeded to chart a course for the son's life, laying down a variety of rules and plans the son was expected to keep, follow, and uphold. How's that for creating tapes in your head? I said, "Yeah, I can believe it. Nothing surprises me anymore."

The Bible has a great deal to say about the tongue and its power. In James 3, the tongue is compared with a rudder on a ship, a bit in a horse's mouth, and a small spark that can set a forest on fire. The tongue might be small, but its power is unmatched. The things people say to us can create deep emotional wounds that direct and destroy our lives if they are not addressed.

What is the most hurtful thing anyone has ever said to you?

____

____

____

____

What is the most hurtful thing you have ever said to your spouse?

____

____

____

____

What is the most hurtful thing your spouse has ever said to you?

____

____

____

____

Things People Do to Us

It's fairly common knowledge that often, although not always, wounded people become wounders. The cycle of abuse and cruelty can continue unchecked generation after generation. The deepest wounds are often perpetrated upon the most vulnerable in our world, the children. Each year, there are hundreds of thousands of reported cases of sexual, physical, and emotional abuse against children in our society. Many other situations go unreported. The majority of men and women in our Hospital Church ministry, who reveal that they were sexually or physically abused as a child, never told anyone about it before coming to our church.

Some statistics report that more than a third of all males and more than half of all females will experience some form of sexual abuse by the time they are eighteen years of age.[2] It's not unlikely that the average pastor on any given Sunday will be speaking to a crowd where the *majority* have suffered the emotional damage of sexual, physical, or emotional abuse in their past. Most have never told anyone about it, much less gotten any help. Why haven't they? Because they never felt it was safe to speak about it and deal with its aftermath in their lives.

2. See for instance: http://www.advocatesforyouth.org/PUBLICATIONS/factsheet/fsabuse1.htm accessed March 2009

If this is true, and the church is not providing appropriate ministry for the healing of those wounds, then we are completely overlooking a vital part of ministry to the total person. So many of the problems that are evident in the marriages and homes of Christians are directly related to these kinds of issues that have never been addressed. Week after week people sit in our churches, covering up the pain of their wounds with a smile and a wave, because the church is not a safe place. That shouldn't be the case.

What is the most hurtful thing anyone has ever done to you?

____

____

____

____

____

____

What is the most hurtful thing you have ever done to your spouse?

____

____

____

____

What is the most hurtful thing your spouse has ever done to you?

____

____

____

____

Things People Take from Us

Losses in life can also be wounding experiences that cause us damage. Losses can take the form of a lost career, or a spouse or other loved one through divorce or death. It might be the loss of a reputation through slander and gossip. Or even the loss of childhood in cases where a child has to grow up far too early in life (I own that one).

The bottom line is, everyone has a pile of garbage. It may be a small pile. It may be a huge pile. One thing is for sure—nobody walks through this world without taking some hits. Those hits create wounds that require specific and strategic healing.

Truth 2: Over Time Our Piles of Garbage Begin to Rot and Stink

Garbage stinks! If you remove it quickly it doesn't have a chance to stink up the house. But if it sits there day after day, it begins to smell—and smell bad. This only makes sense because garbage is made up of the refuse of life. In your garbage at home you deposit banana peels, the ends of the tomato you sliced off, and the leftovers from meals that you couldn't put down the disposal. Garbage stinks!

The emotional piles of garbage we all carry through life also eventually begin to stink. That also makes sense. This pile is also made up of the refuse of life. It's the leftovers of painful experiences and memories, the banana peels, tomato trimmings, and leftovers from the things people have said to us or about us, done to us, and taken from us. As this garbage collects, it also begins to rot and stink. As it rots, it creates an unpleasant environment that affects every aspect of our lives. It needs to be set out by the curb so the collectors can put it where it belongs: the garbage dump.

The tragedy is, while few of us would let a pile of stinking garbage smell up our house for very long, we are often willing to carry this stinking, decaying pile of emotional garbage through our entire lives. Maybe it isn't that we are willing, but have decided we just don't have any choice.

Yet there is another option. We can take the garbage out!

What about you stinks the worst right now to your spouse?

____

____

____

____

What about your spouse stinks the most to you right now?

____

____

____

____

Truth 3: When You Interact with Others, Your Pile Interacts with Their Pile

Since everyone has a pile, then every time you interact with another person, your pile interacts with his or her pile. The effects may be minor, or they may be severe, depending upon the amount of garbage and the nature of the relationship. The more intimate the relationship, the more impact your pile has on that relationship, and vice versa. The deepest impacts are typically seen in the most intimate of all human relationships, marriage.

When two people join themselves in marriage, they also join their individual piles of emotional garbage. Two individual piles are joined to create one giant pile right in the middle of the living room! If they bring particularly sizeable piles into the relationship, the impact begins to be seen very early on and tends to be deeply hurtful. These two people then begin to wound each other in the relationship. Now they are simply adding marriage garbage on top of the individual garbage they brought to the marriage! Over time, as this pile continues to grow, it continues to rot and stink until eventually it is so massive it defines the entire relationship.

This is compounded by the fact that we, often unknowingly, are drawn to people whose particular pile of emotional garbage is especially destructive to us. This is sometimes referred to as the "pathological pull." In simple terms, this means my particular pathology draws me like a magnet to someone who has a pathology that is going to be particularly harmful to me. Another way of saying it is, "A deep unmet need in me seeks out a deep unmet need in you." When we get together, all we have done is to compound the unmet need in both of us. Nothing is made better. Everything is compounded.

For instance, a person who has a strong need for approval will often end up with someone who is emotionally distant and unable, or unwilling, to give healthy approval and affirmation. The person longs for approval, seeks for approval, pushes for approval. The other person moves away or does exactly the opposite of approval and expresses disapproval. Sometimes, a woman who has been abused in one relationship will move into relationship after relationship with abusive men. This pattern makes no sense to anyone, including her. She hates the abuse, but like a moth to the flame she continues to be drawn to men who abuse.

Of course, they abuse because of the emotional garbage they have collected in their lives. They are often simply passing on the abuse they have received. The wounded becomes the wounder. It's a clear expression of the pathological pull. I have seen this cycle demonstrated in the lives of hundreds of people over the last thirty years of pastoral ministry.

What size pile did you bring to the marriage? What are some things in your pile?

____

____

____

____

What size pile did your spouse bring? (in your humble opinion)

____

____

____

____

Truth 4: After Awhile, We Don't Smell Our Own Garbage Anymore

This stage is where the problem of denial really begins to kick in. Perhaps you have seen how this works. After you have lived with a smell long enough, you become immune to it. I grew up in West Texas where the smell of oil can sometimes be overpowering. People who were not from around there would comment about it, but I had breathed it for so long I didn't even notice it. To us, it was normal.

But I'll never forget the experience of driving through the part of Louisiana where the paper mills are. One of my college roommates was getting married and there was a paper mill near the small town where the wedding was to be held. My wife and I drove into that little town and the smell hit us like a ton of bricks. I remember thinking, "How do these people live with this smell?"

Well, the way they live with it is they don't smell it anymore! The technical term is "olfactory desensitization." If you live with a smell long enough, you become desensitized and stop smelling it.

Recently, my wife bought me a little device for my office that is designed to counter olfactory desensitization. I love having fresh scents in my office. I don't care for the musty smell a closed room takes on. She bought me a motorized scent distribution device that is ingenious. It uses a cartridge that has four complementary scents in it. Every thirty minutes it rotates to another scent. Just about the time my nose becomes desensitized to one scent, it changes to another one. That way, all day long, I can smell the fresh and pleasing scents on a rotating basis.

It's an act of the grace of God, for someone living in the West Texas oil fields, or the paper mills of Louisiana, that the scent doesn't rotate every thirty minutes. Nobody could live in either place! But it can be devastating for the person who no longer smells his or her own pile of emotional garbage. The result is the person goes through life blaming all his problems on other people. Here is the crux of the problem. Even though I might not smell my own garbage anymore, I can certainly smell yours! I don't become desensitized to the smell of your garbage. I smell yours just fine!

Jesus indicated this tendency in the Sermon on the Mount when He dealt with the problem of judging. In Matthew 7:3, He said, "Why do you look at the speck that is in your brother's eye, but do not notice the log that is in your own eye?" The simple answer is, "I have lived with this log in my eye for so long that I have developed ways of looking around it. I have lived my life compensating for it for so long that I don't even notice it anymore."

The same holds true when we make the connection between the log in the eye and the pile of emotional garbage in our houses. For instance, here is how it often works itself out in a marriage context. One partner looks at the other and says, "If you would just deal with your garbage, our marriage would be better!" Then they fill in the blank: "If you didn't . . . If you weren't . . .If you would just . . . ." On and on it goes. At the same time, the other partner is saying the same thing in the other direction. Neither of the partners recognizes their garbage because they have lived with it so long they don't smell it anymore. Accusations fly, fingers get pointed, relationships deteriorate into hell.

Where has your focus been up to now in your marriage? Your own garbage or your Spouse's? Explain.

____

____

____

____

____

Which leads to the last truth . . . .

Truth 5: Each of Us Has to Deal with Our Own Pile of Emotional Garbage

More than twenty years ago, the odyssey of a barge called the Mobro 4000 dominated the attention of our entire nation. On March 22, 1987, the Mobro set out on a six-thousand-mile voyage to find a place to dump 3,200 tons of garbage nobody wanted. Do the math—that's a boatload of 6.4 million pounds of stinking garbage!

The trouble all began when the garbage dump in the city of Islip, New York, got full. So the pile was loaded on the Mobro and the ship set out looking for a new home for their garbage. At first it was thought that Morehead City, North Carolina, might take the garbage and turn it into methane fuel. That proved to be a smelly rumor. The Mobro then set off for Louisiana, but Louisiana wanted none of it. Then it was down to Mexico, where the Mexican Navy met the garbage barge in the Yucatan Channel, forbidding it to even enter Mexican waters. Belize also refused to let the Mobro dock. Off to the Bahamas, but the Bahamas wouldn't have it. Before it was over, the Mobro had been rejected by six states, three countries, and had to turn around and go back to New York.

On May 16, after two months at sea, the trash arrived back in New York. But its troubles were still not over. The New Yorkers weren't excited about seeing their garbage show back up on their doorstep. (By this time things were really ripe.) The Mobro wanted to dock near Queens, where the plan was that trucks could carry it back to where it came from in Islip, but the president of the Borough of Queens said not a chance! She didn't even want the garbage to pass through Queens. She obtained a restraining order preventing the barge from even docking. Eventually, in July, the federal government granted the Mobro a federal anchorage in New Jersey. Finally, when all the court challenges had ended, the Mobro made its way back up to Brooklyn, New York, where the garbage was incinerated. On September 1, the first truckload of ash was deposited on the landfill in Islip where five months earlier it had been launched out to sea in hopes that it might become someone else's problem.

And that's the moral of the Mobro. In the end, Islip had to deal with its own garbage. At the heart of the Pile Principle is the core value that each of us must, in the end, deal with our own garbage. No one can do it for us.

Here's a ridiculous question: How much sense would it make if I went up and down my block, knocking on doors, asking, "Can I take out your garbage?" while all the while my own garbage was collecting and piling up in my garage. My neighbors might eventually catch on and say something like, "Hey, buddy, why don't you worry about your own garbage and let me take care of mine?"

That would be a good question, because at the end of the day the only garbage any of us is really responsible for is our own. In recovery circles, this is referred to as "keeping your own side of the street clean." Don't always be trying to clean up the other guy's side. Just take care of your own. That's all you are able to do anything about anyway.

Since marriage is the relationship where emotional garbage does its greatest damage, I'll use the illustration of marriage to explain how this works. There are certain issues every marriage must negotiate. For instance, there are the big three that are usually said to be the top three causes of marital discord and divorce: sex, money, and in-laws. Individuals in a marriage have to be at a minimum level of emotional health before they can even begin to negotiate these normal issues of marriage.

This is what often happens. When a couple gets to the point of desperation about one or all three of these issues, they will go to a marriage counselor. This is sometimes the worst thing they can do. I don't mean that good Christian counseling isn't valuable. It certainly is. I mean this couple may not be healthy enough individually to get any value out of the marriage counseling! Especially if the counseling focuses only on the marriage issues. Those are not the real issues. They are simply the presenting problems of the garbage pile that is buried underneath.

The deeper issues relate to their individual piles of emotional garbage they each brought to the relationship. Often a good and wise counselor will recognize this and recommend seeing them as individuals for a time before they continue counseling as a couple. If the counselor does not recognize this, the couple may go for a few sessions, see no progress, and give up. The end result isn't good.

What needs to happen is for each individual to begin to smell his or her own garbage again. Then each individual can begin the work of reducing his or her own pile. This process includes freedom group work, that you are a part of now. My experience is that involvement in a good freedom group with fellow strugglers, where people use biblically based, thought-provoking material under the guidance of a good facilitator, can bring some of the greatest healing of all. When the two people have reduced their individual piles to a reasonable level, then they can come together and begin to address the issues they have created in their marriage.

Over the years, I have seen this truth prove itself many times. The first time I saw it happen was almost three decades ago. One of the guys who had been instrumental in leading me to Christ had been my freshman college roommate. Then we both transferred to Baylor University at the same time. We were in seminary together. I was in his wedding and he was in my wedding. He married a girl from our hometown and everything seemed to be going well. One day, while we were still in seminary, he called me and asked me to come over to their apartment. He informed me that his wife wanted a separation. I was devastated. So was he.

She told him they had individual issues that needed to be dealt with and marriage issues that needed to be addressed. She wanted to separate while they were in the midst of that process. They did separate, and it lasted about six months. During that time, they each reached into the garbage pile and began to deal with their own stuff.

That eventually allowed them to deal with the marriage garbage they had created together. Today, they are as happily married as any couple I know, and they have eight children, so they must have figured something out.

This process is about getting in touch with your own garbage and focusing on reducing your own pile. When two individuals are willing to do this process with the spotlight turned upon himself/herself instead of on the spouse, the sky is the limit for how much healing, restoration, and fulfillment can be theirs in marriage. They can become partners as they originally planned and stop being competitors.

Throughout this process you will be doing things that will allow you to get back in touch with your own garbage you have stopped smelling. This is a good thing because once you see how nasty it is, then you can begin to do something about it. Maybe you are already aware of some of your garbage that you know you need to begin to deal with.

What is some of the garbage you are already aware of and want to deal with in this process? Identify them in the order of the most urgent to the least urgent.

____

____

____

____

What is the most important thing you have learned in this chapter?

____

____

____

____

TABLE TALK

What is the most important thing about you that relates to this chapter that you are going to share with your spouse this week?

____

____

____

____

JOURNAL

4

Partners or Competitors?

For over thirty years, there is one thing I have spoken about to virtually every couple about to get married, and every couple that has come to me because their marriage was in trouble. I usually begin with a question. "When did you stop being partners and become competitors?" I have never had one of them be able to answer the question initially. They simply look at me with a blank stare. But the answer to that question is crucial because for every marriage that gets in trouble, the answer points to the time when things began to go south.

A PROBLEM

We don't get married to compete. We get married because we desire a partner. A life partner. But the sad truth is, many couples quickly devolve into a competition that eventually pulls the marriage apart. I then go on to explain that once you become competitors in marriage you are done. Game, set, match. It's over unless you change that trend and begin to move back into a partnership.

The entire atmosphere of the two relationships is different. You want to dominate a competitor. You want to support a partner. You want to intimidate a competitor. You want to encourage a partner. You want to beat a competitor. You want to build up a partner. You line up across from a competitor and butt heads. You line up beside a partner and hold hands. You walk away from a competitor when the challenge has ended. You walk with a partner to the next challenge. Do you see the differences?

So, how does the partnership become a competition? Typically it happens at the point of expectations and needs. We all come to marriage with expectations. Some we have voiced but most have never been vocalized. We have expectations about what marriage is going to be like, things our spouse is going to do, be, and on and on. Not only that, but we come to marriage with needs. Men have needs and women have needs.

Those needs are not the same and that is part of the problem with expectations. We "expect" that our spouse is going to have basically the same needs we do, therefore he/she will know our needs and it will be easy and natural for him/her to meet our needs. Men and women, husbands and wives, have a completely different hierarchy of needs! They aren't even close! Not even on the same planet! Houston, we have a problem.

So, early on in marriage, when there are unmet expectations and unmet needs, the partners begin to struggle to get their spouse to measure up to their expectations and meet their needs. The games are on. The competition begins. Of course, the natural human response to pressure is to push back. The more one partner pushes back the more the other one pressures and it becomes an escalating cycle of insanity. The couple has begun the struggle to get each other to do and be what they "need" or "expect" them to do and be. Eventually, no one's expectations or needs are met in the relationship. What was entered into with the hope it would be a little slice of heaven has quickly become a half-acre of hell.

What are some of your expectations for marriage that haven't been realized?

___

___

___

___

What are some of your needs in marriage that aren't being met?

___

___

___

___

AN ANSWER

What is the answer? Well, at this point, I will typically explain what the biblical picture of marriage is compared with what we often do with marriage. It's like the difference between a lake that has two rivers flowing into it and two rivers flowing out, and a lake that doesn't. When the amount flowing in and the amount flowing out are equal, then the reservoir is healthy. It can provide a home for fish, birds, and other wildlife. It can provide a place of recreation and enjoyment for activities such as fishing, boating, and swimming for anyone who desires it. It can provide a life-sustaining source of water for surrounding communities. Everything about it is healthy, vital, and useful.

However, if the flow of the river coming into the reservoir dries up, yet the flow of the water going out continues, there is a problem. The reservoir eventually dries up and dies. The fish die, the ducks have no place to land, the people have no place to recreate, and the surrounding communities have no water to drink. Everything the reservoir was intended for cannot happen. It's nothing but desolation and a dry empty hole in the middle of the landscape.

Those two scenarios represent the difference between marriage when it is a partnership and marriage when it becomes a competition. Let me explain. In the first scenario both partners come to marriage with one goal in mind. They want to meet the needs of their spouse-to-be. So the wife-to-be says, "I want to commit my life to discover the needs of my mate and meet his needs. One hundred percent I am giving myself in this relationship for that purpose." The husband-to-be says, "I want to give myself one hundred percent to meet the needs of my wife. I want to discover her needs and meet her needs." Now in this scenario two rivers are flowing into the reservoir and the two rivers flowing out have plenty of life-giving water in them. The reservoir stays full because of the continuing supply of the two in-flowing rivers. Therefore, the needs of everyone and everything that depend upon it are met. Why? Because everyone is giving, not demanding or taking. Needs are being met but nobody is having to demand, struggle, or fight for them. It's the natural result of a full reservoir that has a steady source of supply.

In the other scenario the partners come to the marriage with a different mindset. The wife-to-be says, "I have needs and expectations. I want my husband to meet my needs and expectations." So she takes out of the relationship what she needs. The husband-to-be says, "I have needs and expectations. I want my wife to meet my needs and expectations." So he takes out of the relationship. In this scenario nobody is giving. What is happening? Everybody is taking. The source of supply has been stopped but the outflow continues. For a while at least. Eventually the reservoir is dry and the marriage becomes a dry desolate hole marring the landscape.

Can you guess which one is the biblical picture of marriage? Over and over again, the Scripture talks about how the essence of the Christian life is to give not take. It is to serve not be served. It is to put the needs of others ahead of our own. To be great Jesus said become the least. To be exalted, be humbled. To be blessed, be broken. To be filled, be emptied. To receive, give! To gain your life, lose it. In essence, the Scripture teaches us to focus our lives on becoming a source of supply!

Which scenario represents how you came to your marriage in the beginning?

To meet your spouse's needs? Explain.

___

___

___

___

To have your spouse meet your needs? Explain what those are.

___

___

___

___

Describe how it's working out for you.

___

___

___

___

A QUESTION

You say, "But don't I have genuine needs?" Yes, you do, and God is interested in having those needs met in marriage. The question is only about how it gets done. Are your needs intended to be met by demanding or giving? That is the crucial question. When both parties in marriage understand God's purpose for marriage and submit themselves to that purpose, then everyone's needs are met but no one has to fight and struggle and demand! Her needs are met and his needs are met because the two are partners not competitors! Both are pouring into the relationship one hundred percent for the other and the needs are met, the reservoir stays full and provides a wonderful and beautiful source of life-giving supply for all who need it.

In fact, the Scripture even addresses this principle directly when it comes to the sexual relationship in marriage. The principle given applies to every need in marriage but the particular situation in the church in Corinth required specific instruction in the sexual relationship between husband and wife.

> *The husband must fulfill his duty to his wife, and likewise also the wife to her husband. The wife does not have authority over her own body, but the husband does; and likewise also the husband does not have authority over his own body, but the wife does. (1 Corinthians 7:3–4)*

That is about as clear as it can be. The wife is to meet the needs of the husband and the husband is to meet the needs of the wife. If this breaks down on either side of the equation, there is going to be trouble in paradise!

A key goal of *Life Change for Couples* is to turn competitors back into partners. This is why both partners in marriage are required to go through this process. It takes two to make this work. So, now the sixty-four-thousand-dollar question is . . .

When and how did you and your spouse stop being partners and become competitors?

____

____

____

____

What effect has that had on your relationship?

____

____

____

____

____

____

A SURVEY

I want to perform a survey to find out just how much we understand our spouse's needs. First, let's find out how in touch we are with our own needs. Then I'll have you list what you think are the top five needs of your spouse.

My Top Five Needs Are:

____

____

____

____

____

____

My Spouse's Top Five Needs Are:

____

____

____

____

____

In my wedding ceremony, that I have used for over thirty years, no matter how many changes I make to it to fit it to the specific couple I am performing the ceremony for, there is a question I always ask the couple individually. I ask, "Are you willing to make whatever adjustment and whatever growth is necessary so that you may genuinely share you life with ________________________?"

I ask it to the groom and I ask it to the bride. So now I am asking you. Are you willing to make whatever adjustment and whatever growth is necessary so that you may genuinely share your life with ________________________?

If you answered yes to that question, write some adjustments and some areas of growth you already know need to happen within you.

In his excellent book, *His Needs Her Needs,*[1] Dr. Willard Harley identifies what he has discovered in his practice as a therapist are the top five needs of a wife and the top five needs of a husband. These are generalizations, and there may sometimes be exceptions, but in general these seem to be true.

The Top Five Needs of a Wife:

1. Affection—Guys, for her this does not mean sex!
2. Honesty and openness—She needs to be able to trust him.
3. Conversation—She needs him to talk to her.
4. Enough money to live comfortably. She needs to know he is doing all he can to provide. When she does, she is more than willing to help out.
5. Family support—She needs him to be a good father.

The Top Five Needs of a Husband:

1. Sexual fulfillment—This one didn't take anyone by surprise, did it?
2. Recreational companionship—He needs her to be his playmate.
3. An attractive spouse—He wants her to care about her appearance.
4. Domestic support—He needs peace and quiet.
5. Admiration—He needs her to be proud of him.

1. Willard H. Harley, *His Needs Her Needs* (Old Tappan, NJ: Fleming H. Revell, 1986).

Compare these two lists. How close were you when it came to listing your own needs?

____

____

____

____

How close were you in your list of your spouse's needs?

____

____

____

____

What is the most important thing you have learned in this chapter?

____

____

____

____

What do you intend to do this week as a result of this understanding?

____

____

____

____

What is one need of your spouse you will commit to begin meeting immediately?

____

In what specific way do you plan to do that?

____

____

____

____

TABLE TALK

What is the most important thing about you that relates to this chapter, that you are going to share with your spouse this week?

____

____

____

____

Chapter 4

JOURNAL

5

"A"—Admit Powerlessness

"We admitted that we were powerless over (spouse's name) and that our lives had become unmanageable."

THE PROBLEM OF "A"

The highest hurdle most of us face in experiencing life change is the first one we face. Admitting there's a problem! That seems to be a huge problem for most of us. Then, after we admit we have a problem, we have to accept that we are powerless within ourselves to do anything about it! That is scary, and can be overwhelming, to say the least. Behind it all is the basic issue of control.

We want to be in control. This desire is what the Bible refers to as the "sin nature." The desire to be in control constantly puts us at odds with situations, other people, and even God. The truth is, most of us spend our lives trying to control situations to get what we want. We try to control people to get them to do what we want and we try to control God to get Him to be and do what we want! Deep down, each one of us has the desire to be God! Immediately when you read that you probably think, "That's not true! I don't want to be God! That's a huge job!" You are right—it is a huge job, but the facts tend to prove that deep down in our fallen human nature that is really what each of us is striving to be.

It all began with our spiritual ancestors, Adam and Eve. The Creator had given the first man and woman all they needed for a happy and fulfilling life. Think about it! A beautiful environment, a perfect life mate, and totally naked! What could possibly be better than that? On top of it all, they had totally unhindered access to, and relationship with, their loving Creator. All they had to do was accept the boundaries that He, in His godly wisdom, had set up. It all worked well for a while, until they were deceived into thinking maybe they knew a better way. That was when they crossed the boundaries that God had set up. In essence, Adam said, "I think I would make a better God than God!" When he decided that, he put himself on a downhill slide. He lost the beautiful garden, his life mate wasn't so perfect anymore, and he had to put on clothes! To top it all off, he no longer had unhindered fellowship with his Creator. We have been living with the results of that decision and repeating the same mistakes ever since.

The result always has been, and always will be, pain and frustration. Perhaps you have experienced the frustration of being called upon to do something for which you were totally unqualified. That's painful and frustrating isn't it? It's like being asked to teach a class on astrophysics and you barely got out of high school biology! In that scenario you have two choices. You can admit that you know absolutely nothing about astrophysics and defer to someone who is qualified, or you can try to bluff your way through. You can easily see where that would ultimately lead—frustration and total failure. Our unwillingness to admit we make a pretty lousy god for ourselves and for others, leads us ultimately to frustration and total failure. On the flip side, when we are willing to admit we haven't done a very good job as the god of our lives, it leads to the immediate help of God. He gives grace when we step out of our pride.

God is opposed to the proud, but gives grace to the humble. (James 4:6)

This passage of Scripture has a pretty sobering message. Friendship with the world means to be in league with the world system, which opposes the control of God. It basically says, "As long as I operate by trying to be God, by trying to be in control, the real God is in opposition to me." In other words, He is working actively against my pride and my god complex! He does this because I have openly declared war against Him to dethrone Him. Now, you may not have seen your compulsion to control as a declaration of war against God, but He sees it that way. The Bible goes on to say that the moment I give up trying to be God, He immediately gives grace! When I declare surrender, He immediately gives grace to begin the rebuilding process in my life.

1. We Try to Control How Others See Us (Image Management)

In our minds, we have an image we want others to have of us, so we work to project that image. We decide in our minds what we want others to think we are and then we set out on a life of image control. In essence, we wear a mask on the outside that doesn't really reflect what we feel on the inside. This lifestyle causes incredible internal tension and in the long run can lead to self-destruction.

Acts 5 tells the story of Ananias and Sapphira and the results of their attempt at image control. They wanted to be seen as incredibly generous, just as people saw another man named Barnabas. Barnabas had sold a piece of land and given every cent of the proceeds to the apostles to be used to help people who were in need. So Ananias and Sapphira went out and sold a piece of land they had and brought the proceeds to the apostles just like Barnabas had done. The difference was that they secretly kept back some of the proceeds. Keeping some of the proceeds wasn't a problem. They weren't required to sell the land or to give all of it to the apostles. The problem was, they wanted people to think they had given it all! They were managing their image by lying and the results in that case were devastating.

What is there about you that you are afraid for others to know?

____

____

____

____

How have you managed your image?

____

____

____

____

2. We Try to Control God (God Management)

Now this one is really kind of subtle. Trying to control God is done when we manipulate our image of who He is in order to justify some action in our life! For example, if sexual promiscuity is something we want to justify, then we just reinvent God by saying, "Well, I know the Bible says sex is meant only within marriage but, hey, God created me with this incredible sex drive so He understands."

Some people try to control God by performance. They think, "Well, if I just do enough good things then that will cancel out all the bad things I want to hang onto!" So, we just try to bribe God or manipulate His image to fit our lifestyle. The problem is, we can't change God. Our attempts to control Him simply result in our missing out on the blessing of knowing Him as He really is. As we have already seen, that puts us at war with Him!

What are some of your thoughts about God that have been attempts to control Him?

____

____

____

____

3. We Try to Control Others (People Management)

This simply means we go through life trying to get others to do what we want them to do or be what we want them to be. There are many tools we use to control and manipulate people and by doing that we try to be God in their lives. Sometimes we do it by outright telling people everything we think they should be doing! Someone said, "I think that everybody has the right to my opinion!" This doesn't mean we should never give our opinion or give input into the lives of people, but a little bit does go a long way. Sometimes we use devices like shame, guilt, fear, and even flattery to get people to do what we want them to do. The focus for this process is often our spouse. So we need to ask ourselves a few questions.

What ways have you attempted to control or change your spouse?

____

____

____

____

What tools have you used (guilt, fear, shame, intimidation, etc)?

____

____

____

____

How has your spouse attempted to control you?

____

____

____

____

What consequences have you seen from that behavior?

____

____

____

____

THE PROCESS OF "A"

Define Powerlessness

Admitting I am powerless doesn't mean there is nothing I can do. I can do plenty. In fact, I am not powerless to control my image, or other people, or even to think I am controlling God. What it means is I am powerless to "effectively" control anything. To "effectively" control means to do so with a positive outcome. I can control myself and others for a while, but in the end the results are always bad. For instance, I can control my children for a long time, but eventually they will resent me for it. When they are able, they may go away and not want to come back. Did I control them? Yes. Did I "effectively" control them? No. Why? Because I didn't get a good result.

I can sometimes control my spouse and make her do what I want her to do against her will, but not "effectively." Not with a good result. Not with a healthy result in the relationship. I can control how people view me . . . for a while. Not effectively. Eventually people see through the image and figure me out. We fool ourselves into believing that because we are technically "powerful" (able) to accomplish all these things then we can get away with control in all its forms and thus are not "powerless." But that is a lie. Time and truth do walk hand in hand. Eventually the truth always is revealed.

How have you seen your attempts to control your spouse prove to be "ineffective"?

____

____

____

____

How have they contributed to "unmanageability" in your life and in your relationship to your spouse (i.e., how has it worked out for you)?

____

____

____

____

____

Admit Powerlessness

The journey you are beginning is about "change." Something has brought you to the place of being willing to begin this journey. The sad truth is that people are incredibly resistant to change. In fact, the willingness to change usually only comes as a result of pain. When the pain gets bad enough, then we are willing to change and reverse our course.

The pain that makes us willing to accept change may come from something we do over and over again, hoping we will get a different result. It may be that the pain comes from allowing someone else to do something to us over and over again.

Einstein's definition of insanity: "Doing the same thing over and over again expecting to get a different result."

The cycle repeats itself until at some point the pain becomes great enough to bring us to the point of admitting, "I can't do this anymore," or, "I don't want to be like this anymore," or "I can't live like this anymore," and we begin to look for help. This is the place of surrender.

What kind of pain is it that has brought you to this point?

____

____

____

____

Pain is a God-given signal that something is wrong. Without physical pain, we wouldn't know to remove our hand from a burning stove, or that we had cut ourselves. The result could be that we might bleed to death. Physical pain tells us to remove ourselves from the cause of the pain. Emotional pain works in the same way. It tells us something is wrong! Then we must choose how we will deal with the pain. We can choose to deal with the issue that is causing the pain, or we can choose to medicate the pain with drugs, alcohol, food, sex, lying, compulsive behavior, or control, and the list goes on and on. Those are all attempts to escape the pain without dealing with the cause. If we did that with physical pain it would kill us. It would be like holding your hand on a burning stove and taking a painkiller to deaden the pain! That doesn't make much sense, does it? The smart thing to do is to remove your hand! In the long run, simply medicating emotional pain will also have devastating results.

The first step addresses two key issues we must face: powerlessness and unmanageability. If your pain has become intense enough, then you are ready to face these two issues. If you are willing to do that, there is nothing ahead for you but hope and growth. Being willing to admit our need and our pain is a major acknowledgement.

Nobody wants to accept they have been wrong. Nobody wants to admit helplessness. But, it is at the point of acceptance of powerlessness that we begin to peel back the layers of denial and self-sufficiency and take our first step into reality and hope.

Truth: When we come to the end of ourselves, we come to the beginning of God. When we come to the beginning of God, we come to the beginning of hope.

The struggle we have with this admission is the basic problem we addressed earlier. We want to be God! We want to be in control! We want to control others, situations, and our projected image (how others see us) and, as we have pointed out, we want to control God by manipulating our image of Him to justify our actions. Jesus said it this way:

"Blessed are the poor in spirit, for theirs is the kingdom of heaven." (Matthew 5:3)

Jesus doesn't mean to be "poor spirited." He doesn't mean to be "poor mouthed." "Poor in spirit" means to give up your self-sufficiency. It means to come to the end of yourself and admit that you are powerless to control life.

What does it mean to you to give up your self-sufficiency?

____

____

____

____

What are some areas where you have operated in your own self-sufficiency and the results haven't been what you would like them to be (relationships, destructive behaviors, lying, guilt, shame, finances, etc.)?

____

____

____

____

What kinds of problems have these behaviors created in your life, which up to this point, you have justified and excused (specifically at home)?

____

____

____

____

Admitting powerlessness means we are admitting our weakness. It may sound like a contradiction to say we must be weak before we can become strong, but that is exactly what the Bible tells us.

> *And He has said to me, "My grace is sufficient for you, for power is perfected in weakness." Most gladly, therefore, I will rather boast about my weaknesses, so that the power of Christ may dwell in me. Therefore I am well content with weaknesses, with insults, with distresses, with persecutions, with difficulties, for Christ's sake; for when I am weak, then I am strong. (2 Corinthians 12:9–10)*

What does the statement, "When I am weak, then I am strong," mean to you?

____

____

____

____

The Bible gives a powerful illustration of the danger of refusing to recognize and admit weakness in Judges 16:1–31. Samson was one of those Old Testament characters who had taken a Nazirite vow of devotion to God. As a sign of the vow, Nazirites were not allowed to cut their hair. Now God had invested great strength in Samson which would remain as long as he didn't cut his hair. But Samson's enemies wanted to learn the secret of his physical strength so they could defeat him. They accomplished this by exploiting a weakness Samson didn't recognize—his desire for women. Not exactly the first or last man to have that weakness! Through it, however, his secret was revealed and his enemies were able to capture him. Samson's self-deception made him careless and vulnerable. Had he been willing to admit he was weak in that area, he could have put up safeguards to transform an area of weakness into an area of strength.

Are there areas of your life that have caused you problems over and over, but you have not been willing to admit your weakness in those areas?

____

____

____

How have those behaviors, emotions, or habits caused your life to be unmanageable?

____

____

____

____

Truth: The things we are unwilling to admit as weaknesses in our lives are the very things that ultimately lead us into bondage.

Samson was captured because of a weakness he wouldn't recognize in his life. Below are listed some things that indicate problems. These areas can be red flags that warn us that perhaps we have already been taken captive by some weakness that we have been unwilling or unable to deal with up to this point.

Alert: Red Flags of Warning

1. Internal Reactions

Internal emotions that seem to overpower us at times, or maybe all the time. Emotions such as anger, fear, guilt, resentments, shame, worry, anxiety, etc.

List some of your internal reactions. A repeated internal reaction indicates a problem!

____

____

____

____

2. External Dependencies

Things that we find ourselves depending upon for a sense of security, happiness, or to escape from pain. Things such as addictions, compulsive behaviors, money, people, status, material things, etc. These are dependencies because they are things we keep going back to when we want relief from stress or pain.

List some of your external dependencies:

____

____

____

____

3. Infernal Actions

Actions that we keep going back to, but we feel are wrong, and afterward they make us feel bad about ourselves. Things such as sexual promiscuity, lying, selfish ambitions, physical violence, cheating, stealing, eating, etc.

What are some of your infernal actions:

____

____

____

____

Real and lasting change comes from the inside. Our usual tendency is to try to find solutions to our problems by changing the external conditions, people, or places we believe are causing our problem. The failure of that approach is it doesn't recognize that the problem isn't outside of us. It's an internal problem. No matter where we go, or what external change we make, we still carry ourselves with us! As long as we remain the same on the inside, then the problem is going to eventually resurface. The act of looking inside makes real and lasting change possible.

> *"For there is no good tree which produces bad fruit, nor, on the other hand, a bad tree which produces good fruit. For each tree is known by its own fruit." (Luke 6:43–44a)*

Fruit is an external expression of the internal nature of the tree. In other words, the fruit flows from the nature of the tree. If we are bearing fruit in our lives that we don't like and has caused us difficulty, the way to change the fruit isn't by looking outside for a reason the fruit is there. The way to bring change is by looking inside.

Make a list of things in your marriage you are willing to admit you are powerless over.

____

____

____

____

If you have been willing to admit your "weakness" in these areas, then you are at a place where God's power can begin to make you strong. What is the most valuable thing you have learned in this step?

____

____

____

____

What do you intend to do in your marriage this week as a result of this step?

____

____

____

____

TABLE TALK

What is the most important thing about you, that relates to this chapter, that you are going to share with your spouse this week?

____

____

____

____

Chapter 5

JOURNAL

6

"B"—Believe the Truth

"We came to believe that a power greater than ourselves could restore us to sanity."

THE PROBLEM OF "B"

Each step of the change process presents its own unique challenges. The first challenge of this step is somewhat of a continuation of the first part of the journey. In the first step, we talked briefly about the insanity of some of our behaviors. We addressed admitting that insanity. Maybe you were ready in that first step to come clean with all of it . . . and maybe you weren't. So in this step, we will go deeper into looking at insane behavior. That challenge will continue.

However, the main challenge of this step comes from another source: what we believe. Not just what we believe about God, but about ourselves, our spouse, our actions, and our feelings. Although this step addresses specifically our belief in God, it really extends to what we believe in every area of life. For some people, the idea of believing in God is not a challenge at all. They accept the existence of God as a given. They have never even considered the possibility He doesn't exist. Their challenge is on a different level from the person who has difficulty even believing there is a God.

True atheists are pretty scarce, yet we who profess belief in God often live our lives as "practical" atheists. In other words, while we say we believe in God, we live as if He doesn't exist.

Truth: The greatest challenge for most people isn't believing in God. It is the God in whom we believe.

You see, along the way in life we sometimes pick up baggage regarding the nature and character of God, and that baggage prevents us from coming to know and trust Him as He really is. There are about as many ideas, thoughts, and beliefs about the character and nature of God as there are people. It doesn't do much good to say we believe in God, if on closer inspection, our perspective of His nature is warped and twisted.

Through this step and the next, we will be dealing directly with what we believe about God, as well as what we believe about everything in life. This will be a great challenge for some of us because our caricatures of God have been with us for a long time. If you have lived your entire life with these misunderstandings of God, they will not be shattered easily. Not only that, but the sources from which most of us got our images of God also make it difficult to let them go. After all, you probably got most of your ideas about God from your parents or from church! Those are two major authoritative sources in our lives. If mom and dad believed this, or if this is what the church I grew up in taught about God, then it must be correct. Right? Wrong! It may very well have been correct, and then again, it may have been warped and twisted.

So, the great challenge of this step is to begin to think correctly about God, self, others, and life. But first, about God. If He is going to be able to do in our lives the good things He desires to do, and that we need Him to do, we must be clear and correct about who He is. When our thinking about God is correct and healthy, then we are able to know Him intimately, trust Him, and receive healing from Him. That opens the door for Him to teach us how to experience the most from every relationship. Particularly marriage. God bless you as you do this leg of the journey.

Write down a few words that describe what you believe about God.

____

____

____

____

____

____

____

____

About yourself

____

____

____

About your spouse

____

____

____

About life

____

____

____

Before this step is finished, you will have some tools to determine what you really believe. At the end, you can come back to what you wrote and see if your thinking has changed, or needs to change in any way.

THE PROCESS OF "B"

We Came to Believe

For this leg of the journey, I want to use Chuck's story as a basic outline. Chuck has been a dear friend and partner in ministry for twenty years. He is now in his seventies. It was late in life when Chuck "came to believe." Chuck's story indicates a process we must go through in order to complete this step of coming to belief. Everyone must come to this step with an open mind and an open heart. It's difficult to look at ourselves with objectivity, much less look at God objectively. Our perception of who God is has been clouded by life experience, opinion, and the important people in our lives, just as much as our perception of who we are has been clouded by those same influences. Those clouds have to be penetrated and we have to come to see Him as He really is before we can come into the intimate relationship with Him He desires to have with us. The only requirement at this point is a willingness to believe. Many others have gone before who began at the point of "willingness to believe" and have found that God is willing to reveal Himself when we are simply willing to believe. Perhaps you have seen the change in the lives of others who have been willing to believe, and those changes have encouraged you to become involved in this process. The challenge now, as we move through this part of the process, is to attempt to look at God with new eyes, a new heart, and allow Him to reveal Himself to you as He really is. If we begin to make that discovery in this step, we will have taken the most important step we could take toward life change and growth. Many years ago, Chuck explained his process and its various stages to me.

A Willingness to Believe

It almost goes without saying, but in order to believe, you must first be willing to believe. In other words, you must "come." This statement addresses the issue of attitude. The truth is, for all of us the heart of the problem is a problem of the heart. For whatever reason (and they are many and varied), some do not believe because they have built up walls against belief. There is nothing wrong with having questions, even doubts, about God! There are answers to most of your questions, and God is big enough to handle all your doubts.

> **Truth: The issue isn't whether you have questions or doubts but what kind of doubter you are.**

There are basically two kinds of doubters:

1. The Honest Doubter

The honest doubter says, "I have some doubts, but I am willing to believe." In other words, the honest doubter is genuinely open to discussion and has no inherent bias against belief! God promises to reveal Himself to those who genuinely seek Him with an open heart and mind.

> *And you will seek Me and find Me when you search for Me with all your heart. (Jeremiah 29:13)*

2. The Dishonest Doubter

The dishonest doubter is the person who has doubts, but deep down inside doesn't really want to believe. In other words, his/her search is not an honest search. The dishonest doubter often loves to debate issues about God, but no matter how many answers are given to his questions, he will not believe because he doesn't want to believe.

He may not even consciously realize his bias against belief because he has lived with it for so long. The Bible calls that a hardened heart.

> *How blessed is the man who fears always, But he who hardens his heart will fall into calamity. (Proverbs 28:14)*

However, if at this point you are willing to believe, God is gracious and patient. He will nourish that willingness as a "mustard seed" of faith. He is so patient that He does not require us to have giant faith to begin the process. Jesus said in Matthew 17:20 that even "mustard seed" faith could move mountains. Even the faith as small as a willingness to believe can be used by God to begin moving the mountains in your life. The truth is, God is not only able to help us in our lives, but He is willing. He wants to come to your aid, but you must first be willing to allow Him to help.

What kind of doubter are you? An honest or dishonest doubter? Explain.

____

____

____

How did you come by your doubts and questions (bad experiences in life, teaching, church, parents, etc.)?

____

____

____

What are some of your doubts?

____

____

____

____

If you are willing to believe, write your willingness in a statement to God.

____

____

____

____

A Wanting to Believe

This part of the step brings us back to what we began in the first leg of the adventure. We must come to the place where, regardless of whether we are ready to admit there is a God who will help us, we are at least willing to admit we have not done a very good job of being the god of our own life. In the past, we have wanted to be God, and now our wants have changed. Or, our wants haven't changed yet and the most we can say is, "I want to want to." God can work with even that much desire.

This speaks to the issue of admitting the insanity in our lives. Remember the definition of insanity is "doing the same thing over and over expecting to get a different result." It doesn't make much sense to keep doing the same thing over and over when it continues to have negative results in our lives. But that is what we often do! For change to happen, we have to want to change or at least "want to want" to change. You might say, "I don't know if I want change, but I'm so sick of what has been happening that I would like to 'want to want' change."

Imagine Bob walking across a dark, remote parking lot to get his car. Just as he is putting his key into the lock to open the door, a man wearing a mask and brandishing a sharp knife boldly approaches him. The masked man cuts Bob, takes all his money, and leaves him there. The next night Bob crosses the same dark and remote parking lot to get his car and the masked man with a sharp knife cuts him and takes all his money again. You would think after two nights in a row Bob would see a connection between parking out in that dark, remote parking lot and experiencing pain and loss. But on the third night, he does it all over again! Any rational person who heard that story would label Bob's behavior insane. You'd want to say to him, "Hey, Bob, if you keep doing the same thing you're going to keep getting the same result—pain."

The reality is, our behaviors are often just as insane. We go through life repeating the same behavior patterns that have in the past always resulted in pain. But somehow we hope to get a different result. We never do. It always results in destructive pain like the man in the story. But there is another kind of pain. Good pain. Pain that results in healing. Let's continue our story but with a few changes.

Now imagine Bob is in the hospital about to have surgery to remove a tumor growing inside his body. A surgeon strides in wearing a mask and carrying a sharp knife; he cuts Bob and then takes all of his money. (Surgery is expensive!) It's painful, but the result of this pain is healing. It's temporary pain for the purpose of bringing ultimate healing. There is bad pain (no healing), and good pain (which brings healing).

So our choice is either to keep going through the pain of our insane behaviors, or to go through the pain of facing our destructive thoughts and actions once and for all (like surgery) and find healing. Either way is painful. The first one is painful indefinitely. The second is painful for a period of time but then is followed by healing and health. The first is "bad pain." The second is "good pain."

Truth: Our insane behaviors over time bring devastating results in our lives and the lives of those who are close to us.

We must be willing to believe. We must be willing to accept that some of our behavior is insane. We must accept that some of the things we have been doing over and over have continued to produce the same results and those results have not been good. In fact, they may have been a broken marriage or marriages. Or, broken relationships with our children and work associates. Maybe the behaviors are beginning to take a physical toll on our body. Certainly the behaviors have brought internal pain, guilt, and shame. The question is, are we willing to see the behavior as it really is—self-defeating and destructive?

Think with me through some real-life illustrations of destructive, "insane" behavior. We are all wired to desire mutually caring and giving relationships. We want our spouse to love us, and we want to express love to our spouse. This is a basic human need. So what do we do? We try to manipulate and control our spouses to get them to do what we want them to do. People don't like to be controlled, so they begin to pull away from us. We respond by trying harder to control them and manipulate them in order to hold on to them. This only causes them to pull further and further away from us. We end up doing more of the very thing that produces the opposite result that we desire. Insane? I think so.

It's normal to eat three meals a day to get the proper nutrition to live. But perhaps we are a little overweight and are depressed about that. So what do we do? We eat! Then we get more depressed because we gain more weight and that causes us to eat more—and on and on. Is that insane? You tell me.

The other extreme is, we eat and then we stick our finger down our throat so we can throw it back up. Then we get to the point where we can't eat anything and keep it down, and our body becomes so decimated that organs begin to shut down. But we keep up the same behavior. Is that insanity?

Maybe we were abused as a child or our emotional needs were not met in our early years. Throughout our life, we have sought to have those emotional needs met through relationships, but over and over we seem to be attracted to people who continue to abuse us in one way or another. Not just physically, but perhaps emotionally and even spiritually. Is that insane?

How about this one? We drink ourselves into a stupor at night and wake up the next day hugging the porcelain god (the toilet). We say to ourselves, "I am so embarrassed about what I might have done or said last night, and I feel so bad right now. If I just live through this morning, I'll never drink again." But, before the clock has gone around one full revolution, we are back at the bottle again. Is that insane?

Maybe your issue isn't with alcohol or chemical abuse. We could go on and on and fill this entire workbook with illustrations of insane behaviors. Perhaps it's time for you to think about your own life. Are there any of these kinds of self-defeating behaviors in your life? Can you be honest enough with yourself to see the patterns? If you can, carefully think through the next two questions.

What are some of the self-defeating behaviors in your life you keep repeating? (destructive relationships, gambling, compulsive lying, overeating, drugs or alcohol, pride, lust, envy, worry, fear, anger, etc.)

____

____

____

____

What are the negative effects in your life (guilt, shame, divorce, health, career, etc.)?

____

____

____

____

A Way to Believe

Now we come to the real crux of the issue. For most people, at least in America, believing in God or wanting to believe isn't a problem. As I said earlier, often the problem is the god we believe in. Wanting to change isn't the problem. Most often, the problem is *how* to change. The how-to is what we are focusing on in this chapter. Along the way in life, we often pick up false ideas and false images of God. In actuality, these images are most often caricatures of God. Have you ever been to one of those theme parks or amusement parks where they have artists who will draw a chalk picture of you in about fifteen minutes? When the artist is finished and you get a look at the drawing, it's shocking! There are enough similarities that you can tell it's you, but it is a very strange-looking you! Your distinctive features have been emphasized and exaggerated to the extent that the result is comical, and maybe even a little insulting. If you have a rather big *schnoz*, then by the time the artist gets through, you look like Pinocchio. If your eyes are a little more prominent than most, when the artist is through, you look like one of those bug-eyed fish. If you have ears that stand out there and catch sound waves very effectively, when the artist is through you look like Dumbo! It's called a caricature.

The point is, there is some truth in the picture, but the truth has been distorted to the extent that it has become a lie! You have a nose, but you aren't just a big nose. You have eyes, but you aren't just two big eyes. You have ears, but you are much more than just two ears. When certain aspects of your physical features are caricatured in this way, it presents a distorted and warped picture of what you really look like. This is exactly what we often do with God. We select particular aspects of His nature and character and focus on them so much that we create a completely distorted view of who He really is. Then we say things like, "If that is who God is, then I don't want to have anything to do with Him!" But, that isn't who He really is. It's just a caricature that has been created in our minds.

You see, every aspect of the nature of God is in perfect balance with every other aspect of His character. If you overemphasize any aspect of His nature, then you distort the true image of who God is. For instance, the Bible says He is a God of love. But then the Bible also says He is a God of justice. In His nature, those two attributes are in perfect harmony. If we overemphasize the love of God and ignore the justice of God, we end up with a caricature of God that is mush! He's just love, love, love, and this is interpreted to mean there is no recompense for ungodly behavior in His creation. If we emphasize the justice of God and ignore His grace and His love, then we end up with a caricature of God as a mean, vindictive dictator, looking to mete out punishment and judgment.

Over forty years ago, J. B. Phillips wrote a little book titled *Your God Is Too Small*. In it, he discusses some common caricatures of God. Any caricature of God is too small. It misses the vastness of who He really is. Below, we have listed some of those caricatures in Phillips's book and a few that don't appear there. Do any of them sound familiar?

1. Resident Policeman

A caricature that portrays God as a giant conscience who is there simply to make people feel guilty. God becomes a cosmic imposer of guilt and judgment. He's like the resident policeman, waiting for us to step out of line so He can hit us with His night-stick. This caricature focuses only on the wrath and judgment of God against sin and ignores the grace and the forgiveness He offers.

2. The Grand Old Man

In this caricature, God is depicted as an old man who may have been fine for His day but who is so far out of step with modern times and the demands of life today that He is pretty much irrelevant. What He had to say was okay for Bible days, but that stuff is all out of date now. This caricature focuses on the eternal nature of God but ignores His omniscience (all-knowing) and His eternal nature.

3. The Gentle Grandfather

A caricature that pictures God as the kindly grandfather in whose eyes his grandchildren can do no wrong. He only sees our good behavior. He can always be counted on for a half-dollar and a stick of gum. Since He sees no wrong in those whom He loves, recompense for sin is never needed. This caricature focuses on the grace of God but ignores His justice.

4. God-in-a-Box

Perhaps the most commonly held view of God, but the one that is the least-often recognized. This caricature views God as our servant who is there to rescue us when we get into a crisis. When the crisis is over, we can set Him aside until we need Him again. He's like a jack-in-the-box. On one the side of the box is a crank which, when turned, plays the music "Pop Goes the Weasel" until the clown suddenly pops up out of the box. Then you stuff the clown back into the box and turn the crank again. God is caricatured as that clown. I'll turn the crank when I need Him and when I'm through with Him, I'll stuff Him back in the box and put the box back on the shelf. This caricature focuses on the compassionate heart of God and His desire to help those who call upon Him but ignores His lordship.

5. Managing Director

In this caricature, God in all His vastness and awesome power, the Creator of all things, cannot possibly be interested in the details of our insignificant lives. He is occupied with running the affairs of the universe, not with our day-to-day struggles and behaviors. This view of God focuses on His omnipotence (complete power) and transcendence (separateness from creation) but ignores His immanence (nearness).

Can you relate to any of these images of God? If so, which ones?

____

____

____

How do you think you came by this image?

____

____

____

____

How has it affected your life (behavior)?

____

____

____

____

What do you think is wrong with this image of God?

____

____

____

____

These are just a few of the caricatures people have about God. It's enough to get us thinking at least. Are there others that you have developed through the years? Can you give them a name and a description? Spend some time thinking about some of them and write them down, using the questions provided below.

What are some other caricatures you can identify in your view of God?

____

____

____

____

How do you think you came by that view of God?

____

____

____

____

How has it affected your life or behavior?

____

____

____

____

Why What We Believe Is So Important

Why is it so important? Because what we believe is the foundation upon which everything in our lives is built. If the foundation of a house is not stable or is cracked, then no matter what kind of house we build upon it, the house will be unstable. The foundation has to be fixed. Sometimes the problem may be so bad the house has to be torn down, a new foundation poured, and a new house built! In other words, in extreme cases, what we believe is so twisted and wrong that the only answer is what one friend of mine called "the scorched earth" solution. Torch the entire thing! Bring in the bulldozers and take everything to ground level so we can begin again with a new foundation.

Here is a very important principle. Memorize it!

Principle: Every action is preceded by a thought. Every behavior is based upon a belief.

In other words, we act out of what we believe. If there are behaviors that need to be changed, then before long-term change can take place, the wrong belief must be changed! Short-term change can be accomplished without belief change. However, long-term change requires a change in belief. When the belief changes, long-term behavior change can take place. This principle is firmly rooted throughout Scripture.

But if any of you lacks wisdom, let him ask of God, who gives to all generously and without reproach, and it will be given to him. But he must ask in faith without any doubting, for the one who doubts is like the surf of the sea, driven and tossed by the wind. For that man ought not to expect that he will receive anything from the Lord, being a double-minded man, unstable in all his ways. (James 1:5–8)

Unstable faith (belief) results in being tossed back and forth and not receiving from the Lord what we need and He desires to give. We must first believe rightly, and then we must be secure in that belief.

Do not eat the bread of a selfish man, or desire his delicacies; For as he thinks within himself, so he is . . . (Proverbs 23:6–7a)

What does it mean to "think within himself"?

____

____

____

____

Therefore I urge you, brethren, by the mercies of God, to present your bodies a living and holy sacrifice, acceptable to God, which is your spiritual service of worship. And do not be conformed to this world but be transformed by the renewing your mind . . . (Romans 12:1–2a)

What is the way by which we are transformed?

____

____

____

____

What do you think that means?

____

____

____

____

For though we walk in the flesh, we do not war according to the flesh, for the weapons of our warfare are not of the flesh, but divinely powerful for the destruction of fortresses. We are destroying speculations and every lofty thing raised up against the knowledge of God, and we are taking every thought captive to the obedience of Christ . . . (2 Corinthians 10:3–5)

The imagery in this passage is one of war. Over and over in Scripture, we are told that we are involved in a spiritual war between Satan and God. The battleground as presented here is our mind, thoughts, and beliefs. The battle is won or lost based upon who captures our minds. Whichever one wins the battle for our minds (beliefs) controls our behavior.

The Enemy desires to build "fortresses" in our minds and capture our minds. These fortresses are built brick by brick through lies and false beliefs. In fact, that is the only weapon our Enemy has! Lies. Jesus told us that Satan is a liar!

"He was a murderer from the beginning, and does not stand in the truth because there is no truth in him. Whenever he speaks a lie, he speaks from his own nature, for he is a liar and the father of lies." (John 8:44)

All that the Enemy seeks to accomplish in our lives, he does through lies and false beliefs. Lying is what he does because it is who he is at his core. Here is a thought. If Satan's very nature is a lie, then I am never more like him than when I lie. When I lie, I am reflecting the very nature of the Enemy. When I believe a lie about God, myself, or others, I have played into his schemes. What does he seek to accomplish with his lies? Jesus told us.

> *"The thief comes only to steal and kill and destroy; I came that they may have life and have it abundantly." (John 10:10)*

That puts it in plain language. The Enemy, through his lies, seeks to destroy any hope of anyone having the abundant life Jesus wants to give. He is a destroyer! So what is the opposite of a lie? The truth! If lies are the weapons the Enemy uses, then he can only be defeated by truth. Truth is how the battle is won.

> *"You will know the truth and the truth will make you free." (John 8:32)*

Who is the truth? Where is truth found? Who is the source of all truth? Jesus said,

> *"I am the way, and the truth, and the life . . ." (John 14:6)*

This means that Jesus, at His very core and nature is truth. I am never more like Jesus than when I am telling the truth and living according to the truth. When I am telling a lie or living my life according to a lie of the Enemy, I am not reflecting the character of Jesus and therefore cannot experience the abundance He desires me to have.

Now come back to 2 Corinthians 10. Verse 5 says, "We are taking every thought captive to the obedience of Christ." We pull down the stronghold of the Enemy's lies by taking every thought captive to the obedience of Christ. In other words, we have to discover the areas where we have believed a lie of the Enemy about God, ourselves, others, or life, and then replace it with the truth of God. When we do that, our attitudes and behaviors begin to change. Why? Because all behavior is based upon belief. Behavior springs out of belief.

Question: Is it possible to act contrary to what you believe? Yes____No____
Why?

____

____

____

This may seem like a trick question, but it isn't meant to be. The answer is no; it isn't possible. At least not for the long haul. Why? Because all action springs out of belief! The reason that question seems so difficult is because it is possible to act contrary to what you *say* you believe or what you *think* you believe, or what you know you *should* believe, or even *wish you did believe*. But not what you actually believe.

Truth: It is often difficult for us to determine what we really do believe!

We convince ourselves that we believe certain things, but underneath it all there is a lie at the root of our behavior. It's like painting a wall in your home. If you have a mold problem in a wall, you can take one of two courses of action. You can tear the wall out and deal with the mold, or you can paint over the mold. The first course of action will deal with the problem. The second course of action will only cover it up for a little while. Eventually the mold will come through the paint, and then you have to put another coat on to cover it up temporarily. But it always eventually comes through, and the effects of the mold continue to be evident in the smell, sickness, and allergic reactions it causes in the people who are living in the house. Even when it is covered up with paint!

That's what we often do with our beliefs. We cover them up with layers of religious language. We know what we should believe. We know the words and how to communicate the beliefs, but sometimes this is all just layers of paint, covering up what we really believe deep down inside. We have said the right things for so long that we even convince ourselves they are what we believe! However, the effects of the lies are evident in our attitudes and behaviors.

The Curse of Knowledge

In their book *Made to Stick*, authors Chip and Dan Heath talk about the curse of knowledge. Not that knowledge is bad. Knowledge is good, but sometimes we can know so much about a subject that we forget what it was like when we didn't have that knowledge. Then when we talk about the subject it is difficult for the average person to understand us! That is the curse of knowledge. We have to work to speak about our subject without technical jargon that confuses the average person.

In the context of life change, the curse of knowledge has another application. Sometimes we confuse knowing with believing. We think because we know something, it is what we actually believe. Knowing and believing are not the same. In the spiritual realm this is particularly true. We may know God loves us because we have memorized John 3:16 and have quoted it most of our lives. This knowledge, however, is different from *believing* that God loves me personally. In truth, I may have convinced myself that I believe it because I know it. But if I don't relate to God as I would to someone I believe loves me unconditionally, then there is a contradiction between what I know and what I believe. At this point, I must accept that what I know is not what I believe and begin working to discover the lie that has been covered up with all my knowledge.

Principle: If there are behaviors in your life which are contradictory to what you say you believe, or think you believe, that is not what you really believe!

There is a lie underneath the behavior that is the root of the problem. The contradictory behavior is a warning signal that there is a faulty belief hidden deep inside, and you need to go on a digging expedition to discover the lie and replace it with the truth of God. You need to experience a transformation of the mind; a "taking every thought captive to the obedience of Christ" in that particular area. This is the truth that is taught in the book of James when James says faith that doesn't result in works is dead faith. It isn't real. Real faith will result in works that reflect that faith.

Even so faith, if it has no works, is dead . . . (James 2:17)

Principle: If your conviction (belief) isn't reflected in your behavior, it is not a conviction but a contradiction. Contradictions always indicate a deception.

Take a moment to think about some persistent attitudes or behaviors in your life that seem contradictory to what you think you believe. Begin with the behavior. Then list the belief that seems contradictory. Before you begin this, allow me to give you some examples of how subtle this process really is. Read through the examples and then think about your own behaviors.

Example 1

I say I believe God knows what is best in every area of my life. But then I follow that up with the behavior of rarely, if ever, seeking His Word to discover what He says about what I should do in a given situation. Do I believe what I say I believe? Not really. If I did, I would seek Him. So there is a lie somewhere beneath what I say I believe. Maybe the lie is, deep down inside I really believe God has given up on me. Maybe I really believe He is out to get me. He cares for others but not really for me, etc. If I don't really believe God knows what is best for me, then it makes sense I won't seek Him for guidance.

Example 2

I say I believe my spouse is trustworthy. However, I question everything he/she tells me about finances, recreation, relationships, work, etc. Do I really believe what I say I believe, or is that what I know I *should* believe or I would *like* to believe? What does my behavior say about what I really believe?

A personal story. Beginning in the mid 1980s until the early 1990s, I went through a period of extreme personal struggle. I was married, had two beautiful children, was pastoring a church and had completed my education all the way to the doctoral level. But I began spiraling into a deep and dark depression. I had lost almost 20 pounds, couldn't sleep, and was completely miserable. It got to such a drastic point that one Sunday morning I stood up to preach and had to tell the church I just couldn't do it that day.

I walked out and went home and went to bed. The darkness was the result of a great frustration about the type of ministry we were doing tied into childhood emotional woundedness that I had never addressed. Of course, I didn't recognize all of that at the time. I just knew I was nearly dying. Interestingly enough, during this time, I was crying out to God for Him to deliver me from the darkness I was in. I was spending hours praying. I was memorizing books of the Bible, not just verses. Seriously. But I kept getting worse. Years later, when I began to acknowledge the emotional woundedness and the need to address those wounds, I went through a Twelve Step process with my friend, Chuck, whom I mentioned earlier. In the second step of the guidebook, we were using, the first question asked was, "When did you lose faith in God?" When I read that question, I was almost offended by it. I thought, "I have never lost faith in God! I'm a pastor, for goodness' sake!" So this is what I wrote:

> In the early 90s, I was praying and seeking with all that was in me, but continued to spiral down. I didn't lose faith but it hurt.

That was what I wrote. Chuck and I met every week for months and eventually completed the study. Then I started it all over again with a different group of men. When I came to this step the second time, and I read what I had written before, I immediately saw it for what it was. A whitewash. I remember thinking, "That was lame." I had peeled enough layers of the onion back by this point to know that what I had previously written wasn't the truth. However, I still didn't know what the truth was. So I did something I have recommended to people ever since when they are stuck and don't know what to write. I put my pen on the paper and just began to write. What came out of the end of my pen astounded me for its simplicity and its depth. This is what I wrote the second time:

> I have since come to understand that God was not ignoring me or rejecting me but I was still trying to get through it in my own power without humbling myself to others. Sometimes our reaching out to God is not an expression of faith, but an expression of our pride! We don't want to humble ourselves before others, so we try to do it in secret, just between God and us.

I realized in that moment I had been angry with God for not rescuing me when I cried out to Him. At the same time, I realized why He hadn't been able to rescue me. It was because I was so full of pride I wouldn't let others know what was going on inside of me. I was a pastor, and I wanted just God and me to fix it between the two of us so that nobody else would ever know. He had to resist me in my pride. What I was calling "faith" by crying out to Him was really an expression of pride. See how subtle the lies can be? I was calling something "faith" (because I was doing some good things like praying and memorizing Scripture) that was really an expression of pride! I had to see that lie and admit the lie before I could ever come to the truth! Healing is a result of getting to the real truth of what we believe.

I hope these two examples and my personal story illustrate for you how subtle these lies are. So, take some time to do the exercise below. Identify a behavior you don't like in yourself. Then think about what you *believe*. Is there a contradiction between what you say you believe and what you do? Then, what is the lie? First, do this exercise about any area of your life and then there is one question about your marriage.

Behavior ____

Belief that seems contradictory ____________________________

Possible lie ____

Now let's do one that relates specifically to your spouse and your marriage. What is a destructive behavior in your marriage? Focus on one your spouse has pointed out before. What is the belief you say you hold to in that area? Is there a contradiction between that belief and your behavior? If there is, what could the lie possibly be that you truly believe?

Behavior in marriage _____________________________________

Belief that seems contradictory ____________________________

Possible lie ____

Even in this kind of honest attempt at introspection and transparency, our ability to be in denial and cover up the truth becomes evident. That's why this process can be so grueling and takes time. It's like peeling the layers from an onion. With each layer, you may believe you have gotten to the core, only to discover there are more layers to peel back before you get to the core belief. This is difficult work!

Added to this is the fact that things usually get worse before they get better. It requires a strong determination to press through the difficulty in order to get to the change that is on the other side. Below is a diagram to help illustrate the process and its difficulty.

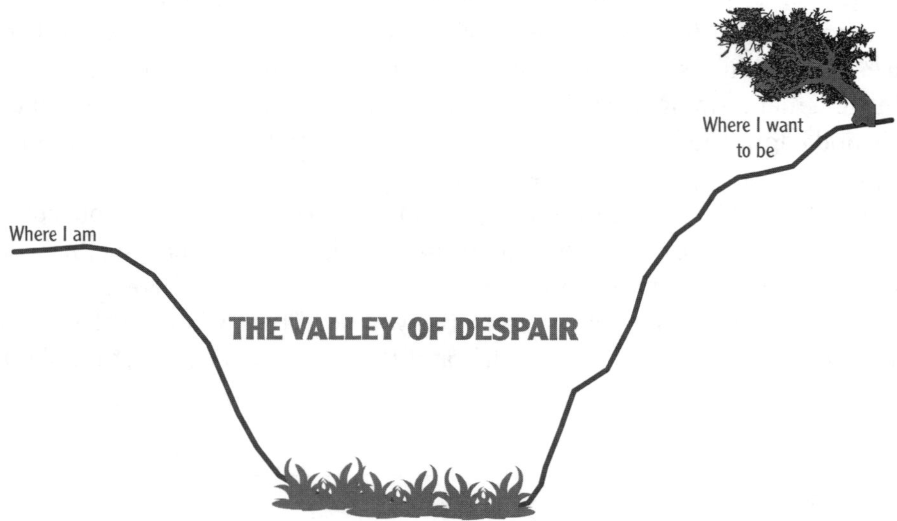

The Valley of Despair

My son has played golf since he was eight years of age. He played golf in college on an athletic scholarship, and at the time I am writing this, is a touring professional. I typically use this diagram to illustrate what a golfer must do in order to improve his golf score. However, it can be used to illustrate any kind of improvement a person desires. It all relates to beliefs. Let me use the golf illustration, and it will be apparent how the principle transfers to our discussion about life change.

In golf, unlike other sports, a lower score is better. Suppose I typically shoot a score of 95 on the golf course. However, the guys I play with regularly shoot around 85. This means every time I play with them, I am getting dominated to the tune of ten strokes. Consequently, I decide I want to lower my score by 10 strokes so I can be competitive with my buddies. Anyone who plays golf knows that in order to take 10 strokes off your score, something has to change. So, I go to a golf instructor for him to analyze my swing. He says, "Well, you are laying the club off at the top and that causes you to come over the top on the downswing, and that is what puts the big left-to-right slice on your ball that causes you to have to play out of the trees so much." He shows me how to make the change, and I'm really excited! The next Saturday on the #1 tee box, I'm bragging about how I've had a lesson and I am going to shoot 85 today! At the end of the round, I didn't shoot 85. I didn't shoot 95. I shot 105! My scored didn't get better, it got worse! There's a lot of laughter and ribbing going on in the 19th hole (the snack bar where we gather to tell lies about the round) that day. I have just entered into the valley of despair.

The next week, I go out and shoot 105 again! Now my buddies are really giving it to me! A lot of trash talking is going on, and I leave the course that day totally frustrated. I'm thinking to myself, "I thought this change was supposed to help me! It's made me even worse than I was!"

This is a critical point in the process. What most golfers do at this point is go back to the old swing that got them a 95 score. They abandon the change. But they go back to the old swing with a determination to shoot an 85 score with that old swing. They work harder at the old swing. The problem is that working harder at something that's wrong doesn't bring better results. If I'm doing the same old thing, I'm going to keep getting the same old results. The fact is, most once-a-week golfers spend their entire golfing life going back and forth in this process. They go to a swing coach and hear the same instruction they have heard before. They try the change on the course and get frustrated and go back to the old swing. They get frustrated with that again, and go back to the swing coach and get the same instruction. The cycle goes on and on. This is why most golfers spend their entire golfing life feeling frustrated. Either frustrated with their score or frustrated trying to make swing changes work for them.

The problem is most golfers are not willing to stay in the valley of despair long enough for the changes to become comfortable and natural. That's when the benefit of the change can be realized. Here is the question: What has to happen in the golfer's belief system in order for him to be willing to stay in the valley long enough to get the benefit of the swing change? First, he has to want the change with everything that is within him, and he has to abandon the belief that he can somehow turn his old swing into something that will yield the result he wants. As long as he holds onto his former belief, even a shadow of it, he will keep going back to it and will never be willing to stay in the valley long enough to get the benefit. Once he abandons the old belief, then he will be able to adopt a new belief, which is the only way possible to get to a better score. He must stay with the change and stay in the valley as long as it takes. This is true of any change whether it is golf or life. Change happens through the valley, and so we must stay in the valley long enough for the change to take place. Things usually get worse before they get better!

So, to change a belief, which in turn results in a change in behavior, there is a five-step process.

Acknowledge the faulty belief—I have to identify the lie.

Abandon the faulty belief—I have to give up on it.

Accept the truth—Find what God has to say about it and agree with that. Take every thought captive to the obedience of Christ.

Act on the truth—I have to practice the new belief until it becomes ingrained. It probably will not be comfortable or easy because it is new. I must stay in the valley long enough for it to become normal.

> *But prove yourselves doers of the word, and not merely hearers who delude themselves. (James 1:22)*

> *"Therefore everyone who hears these words of Mine and acts on them, may be compared to a wise man who built his house on the rock. And the rain fell and the floods came, and the winds blew and slammed against that house; and yet it did not fall, for it had been founded on the rock. Everyone who hears these words of Mine and does not act on them, will be like a foolish man who built his house on the sand. The rain fell, and the floods came, and the winds blew and slammed against that house; and it fell—and great was its fall." (Matthew 7:24–27)*

This is where the will comes in. Stay in the valley and do what is right long enough for it to become a new way of life.

Appreciate the change—Celebrate the blessing! Celebrate the change! Then you can use the memory of that victory and the blessing the next time you have to confront a false belief and go through this process again.

Continuing Assignment

Go back to the list of behaviors, beliefs, and lies you worked through previously and expand it now that you have deeper understanding. Ask yourself, "What do I really believe about . . . ? Is my behavior reflective of that belief?" If not, then what could be the lie beneath what I say I believe? Begin to peel away the layers of the onion until you get to the core. See if you now have more clarification.

This step will not come quickly for most. God is patient and is willing to move us along a step at a time. What areas in Steps 1 and 2 are you having difficulty with so far?

____

____

____

What is one important thing you have learned from this step of the process?

What faulty beliefs about marriage have you been operating by?

What do you intend to do in your marriage this week as a result of this step?

TABLE TALK

What is the most important thing about you that relates to this chapter, that you are going to share with your spouse this week?

JOURNAL

7

"C"—Commit to Christ

"Made the decision to turn our will and our lives over to the care of God."

THE PROBLEM OF "C"

The problem of the third step is overcoming our self-determination and self-will. Even when we come to recognize that our self-will has repeatedly placed our thoughts and actions in places that were not healthy emotionally, spiritually, and even physically, we still struggle to hold onto it. We have built a life around self-determination, and it has become the life that is familiar, comfortable, and safe, even though the results have proven to be destructive in our lives.

The third step challenges us to let go of that self-will and trust in the will of God for our lives. If we have successfully completed the first two steps, then turning our will and the care of our lives over to God is the only logical thing to do. We are not God, although we have tried to live as though we are. We had nothing to do with the creation of the world or anything in it. Everything about creation screams out that there was a great designer. One of the classical arguments for the truth of creation is the garden in the forest. If you are walking in a forest and come upon a well-tended garden, you would assume there was a gardener. The rows are straight, the weeds have been removed, and the plants have been placed in perfect order. There must be a gardener, even though you do not see him when you walk into the garden. Day after day, you walk to that garden and the order and beauty remains, but you never see the gardener. You only see the result of his work. It's certainly more logical to believe he exists, even though you do not see him, than to believe the garden exists in its order and beauty by accident! Everything in our existence illustrates to us that order and design does not happen by accident. Accident always results in chaos not order.

There is a Divine Gardener who created all things, and He does have a purpose and design for all creation, including our lives. It just makes sense. If He created us then His plans and purposes for us would be of more benefit than our own limited and shortsighted plans. In other words, His perfect will and wisdom would be better for us than our own self-will and self-determination. By the time we come to the third step, our lives have proven our self-will has not resulted in much good.

The third step challenges us to begin a new life. We are to forsake the past life of trying to control the universe around us and submit our lives to the One who created all things. We begin a lifelong process of changing from hurting to loving, from fits of rage to patience, from envy to kindness, from selfishness to selflessness, from control to release, from despair to hope. However, we recognize that surrendering our life and will to a God we distrust, or are afraid of, will never work. This is why we began to address our misconceptions about the character of God in the second step. We need to, as Keith Miller says, "Fire that God!"[1] Fire that God that is only a caricature and discover the One and only true and living God who is worthy of our trust and the submission of our lives. The third step moves us one step further in this discovery and then challenges us to make a decision about turning our will and the care of our lives over to that God. In a very homespun way of saying it, "It's time to fish or cut bait" in the third step. This is where the rubber meets the road. We must make this initial decision of the will, and then every day for the rest of our lives we learn to daily make the decision to turn our will and the care of our lives over to Him. We pray that when you have finished this leg of the adventure, you will have made this decision and will be poised to go the distance in healing and hope. That is the Divine Gardener's will and purpose for us all.

THE PROCESS OF "C"

I want to introduce this step in the process with a story that is based upon something Bill Hybels tells in his teaching series on the Twelve Steps. Imagine for a moment you are back in the days when the frontiers of the American West were wild and as yet unsettled. You are traveling across the wild frontier and all of a sudden you come to a great waterfall. Water is rushing over the falls and plummeting hundreds of feet to the river below. There is no way to go forward. Then you look over your shoulder and see a band of Native Americans whose ancestors have lived on that land for centuries and don't appreciate your intrusion. They are coming at full speed and in full war paint right toward you. The air is filled with war whoops and arrows from their bows. You've got the waterfall before you and the unhappy residents of the land behind.

1. Keith Miller, *Hunger for Healing* (New York: HarperCollins, 1991), p. 51.

So what do you do? Well, you get off your horse and begin to prepare a fire to cook dinner! That's denial! You are acting in denial of the reality of your situation. Your life is out of control and unmanageable and you are acting in denial. You are refusing to face facts.

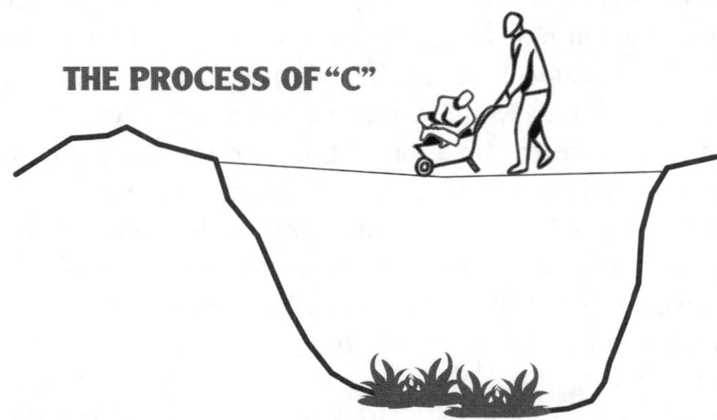

About that time, the arrows begin to fall all around you. One even goes through your ten-gallon cowboy hat and sends it flying. All of a sudden, you realize, "I'm in a tight spot here!" You have just moved beyond Step 1. You have moved out of denial! About that time, you look up river and see the strangest thing. You see a cable strung across the river! All the way across. Not only that, but you see something even more amazing. There is a guy walking across the river on the cable!

So what do you do? You run as fast as you can toward this guy crying out, "Help! Help! Help!" You are at Step 2. You have now begun to look beyond yourself. You have recognized that you need someone else's help to get out of your fix. (By the way, you have time to do this because the Native Americans have stopped at your camp and are now drinking your coffee.) The guy walking on the cable looks at you, turns around, and walks all the way back across the river. He gets a wheelbarrow and pushes it all the way back across the falls with the raging river below. When he gets to your side, he looks at you and says, "You need help, mister?" You reply, "Yes, I need help! I'm in a desperate situation!" He says, "Then get in the wheelbarrow and I'll take you across." You are now at Step 3. It is now decision time. You have to decide if you are willing to place your trust in this person. In essence, you have to commit yourself totally to him. You have to turn it all over to him. If you get in the wheelbarrow, you are giving up control completely. Once you are out there on the wire, sitting in the wheelbarrow, there is nothing you can do but trust. That is both a scary and wonderful place to be. It is scary because we don't like to give up control. It is wonderful because it is at the point of giving up control where we can ultimately find help.

Should you choose not to get in the wheelbarrow? What option is left to you? You can turn and face the angry natives bearing down on you and try to fight it out. Does the name General George Custer mean anything to you? He was made famous by being slaughtered at Little Big Horn. He got his fame, but he had to die to get it. You can choose to face the angry attackers, but you are desperately outnumbered and your chances of success are slim. In fact, turning and fighting in our own strength and with our own resources is what many of us have been doing for a long time, and we have continued to get the same result, failure, and despair.

Surrendering to the God who created you is the only sane choice. I say again, we had nothing to do with the creation of this world. Since He is the Creator and Designer of life, it would seem logical that His plans and infinite wisdom would be of more benefit to our well-being than our finite wisdom and knowledge. To put it another way, our self-centered, self-controlled decisions have resulted in our being at the place where we are today emotionally, relationally, and spiritually. Is that where we desire to stay? If not, then we must be willing to get into the wheelbarrow and turn it all over to Him in trust.

Using the previous story as a guide, think of where you are in your life right now. Are you sitting at the fire in denial? Turning to fight? Ready to get in the wheelbarrow? Explain.

____

____

____

____

At what point in this story do you find yourself in your marriage?

____

____

____

____

Explain:

____

What kinds of feelings do you have when you consider turning your life over to Christ?

Are there areas of your life you would be unwilling to turn over to God?

What would keep you from submitting your life to the care of God?

At this point, maybe it would be best to explain what it means to turn our will over to God. Actually, it's possible to partially submit our will to God and receive part of His benefits, or we can completely submit our will to God and receive all of the benefits He wants to give us. This may sound strange, but I believe it is true. Let me explain.

Partial Submission of Your Will and the Care of Your Life to God

A partial submission would be to decide to merely accept and practice these principles presented in this workbook. They are principles taken from the Bible, God's Word. If we choose to submit ourselves to these truths of God from the Bible, they will work in our lives. For many decades, men and women have been proving this fact in all kinds of support groups for overcoming alcohol addictions, drug addictions, compulsive behaviors, and various other kinds of life-destroying behaviors. They are the truth of God, and truth works when it is practiced. If that is all you are looking for at this time in your life, you can find that kind of help for your life. However, we feel integrity demands we tell you the way to have all God wants you to have.

> **Truth: The way to receive all God has to offer is through surrender of your life to Jesus Christ as Lord and Savior.**

Even this doesn't guarantee you will have the abundant life Jesus offers. Even many Christians don't access all of the things God has to offer. However, surrendering your life to Christ makes it "possible" for you to access all the things God desires for you to have. Understand, if you do not choose to do that, you will still be accepted, loved, and encouraged by this freedom group. Please allow us to tell you about how you can find the fullness of what God wants you to have in Christ.

Complete Surrender of Your Will and the Care of Your Life to God

You may be saying, "Well, I don't have a problem accepting God and practicing these truths I am learning, but I'm not sure about this Jesus thing." Many people have had that initial response when they hear about Christ. Understand, there is a contradiction in that response. As has already been stated, these truths are principles from the Bible, God's Word. That same Bible not only teaches these principles but also clearly says Jesus Christ is the only way to a true relationship with God, abundant life on this earth, and the promise of eternal life when we die.

> *And there is salvation in no one else; for there is no other name under heaven that has been given among men, by which we must be saved. (Acts 4:12)*

If what God has said in these principles from His Word is true, and we are willing to accept and practice these truths and receive benefit from them, then why not remain open to discovering the truth of what the Bible says about Christ and the greater benefit we can receive from a commitment of our life to Him—not only for this life, but for all eternity? This is all we ask you to do. Keep your mind open and be willing to investigate.

You may have many legitimate questions that need to be answered. Questions such as, "Why do I need Christ in order to know God?" "What qualifies Jesus Christ to be my way to God?" "If all of this is true, then how do I make this commitment of my life?" We want to begin to answer those questions in this step.

The idea of turning your life over to a God you don't trust, understand, or are afraid of will likely not work. What are your feelings about doing this? List specific fears and concerns.

____

____

____

____

Sometimes people have said they don't accept that Jesus was the Son of God. They say He was just a good man, a teacher, a prophet, but not the only Son of God sent to earth to pay the price for the sins of mankind. C. S. Lewis, the brilliant Oxford professor of literature who went from being an agnostic to a dedicated believer in Christ, responded eloquently to this statement in his classic work, *Mere Christianity*.

> I am trying to prevent people from saying the really foolish thing that people often say about Him. "I am ready to accept Jesus as a great moral teacher but don't accept His claim to be God." That is the one thing that we must not say. A man who was merely a man and said the sort of things Jesus said would not be a great moral teacher. He would either be a lunatic—on a level with a man who said he was a poached egg—or else a madman or something worse. You can shut him up for a fool. You can spit at Him and kill Him as a demon or you can fall at His feet and call Him Lord and God. But let us not come up with any patronizing nonsense about His being a great human teacher. He has not left that option to us. He did not intend to.

In essence, Lewis is saying that Jesus was either a liar, a lunatic, or who He said He was. Those are the only three options we have. If He said the things He said about Himself, such as being the Son of God and the only way to God, and knew they were not true, then He was a liar. However, the character and quality of His life gives no indication of the kind of person who would be that deceptive. If He said the things

He said about Himself and they were not true, but He believed them to be true, then He was crazy! But again, when you examine the teachings, the life, and the character of Jesus, there is nothing there to indicate that He was a man so out of touch with reality as to have been crazy. The only option left, if you reject the first two, is that He was exactly who He said He was. He was the Son of God, the Savior of the world. He is Lord. This is what we who are Christians believe with everything that is within us. This is what I want to share with you now. To do so, I need to address four issues: God, People, You, Christ. Around these four subjects, the Bible explains how anyone who is willing can come into a personal relationship with Him that will result in power to live in this life and the promise to live forever with God in the next life.

I hope you will at least be open to reading the material and will ask questions about what it means for you.

What Happens When We Turn Our Will and Our Life Over to Him?

The answer is very simple. We begin a process of life change that only God can give and only God can complete. Any of us can change on the outside for a short period of time and sometimes for long periods of time. But only God can bring change from the inside out. This is real and lasting life change. Change on the outside only is like the proverbial "putting lipstick on a pig." It's still a pig. Real and meaningful change happens from the inside out.

> *I urge you therefore, brethren, by the mercies of God, to present your bodies a living and holy sacrifice, acceptable to God, which is your spiritual service of worship. And do not be conformed to this world, but be transformed by the renewing of your mind, that you may prove what the will of God is, that which is good and acceptable and perfect. (Romans 12:1–2)*

1. Submission Begins with a Presentation

The imagery used here is right out of the Old Testament sacrificial system. The Old Testament people would bring a sacrifice to God and present it at the sacrificial altar. This meant that the sacrifice was yielded over to God. Ownership was being transferred. Notice, the passage says it is "your body" that is to be presented. That's interesting, isn't it? Your body. Why the body? Could it be because your body represents the totality of who you are? Everything we do, we do in our body! You probably can't remember the last time you did something without your body. You think, speak, eat, drink, work, recreate, and love in your body. The body represents everything you are. God wants us to turn our entire self over to Him.

With that meaning in mind, take a few moments to write down all of the areas of your life that you can think of that would be included if you presented your body.

2. Presentation Leads to a Transformation

a. Do not be "conformed" to this world

In order to live happy, healthy, whole lives on this planet, a transformation has to take place. Why is this true? Because as we live on this earth, we are wounded by our own sinful choices, as well as the sinful choices of others, that cause hurt and pain. Along the way, because of those hurtful experiences and destructive choices, we develop ways of thinking that are twisted and warped. These ways of thinking lead to ways of living that move us further from the life God desires us to have, and deeper into despair. We investigated the power of what we believe in the last step.

The process we have just described is the pressure we all experience to be "conformed" to this world and its destructive patterns. The word "conformed" is a word that means, in the original language of the New Testament (Greek), "to be squeezed into a mold." Perhaps you have seen a cake maker use an icing bag to decorate a cake. He puts the icing into the bag and then puts a mold on the end of the bag in the shape of whatever he is wanting the icing to look like. He then begins to squeeze the bag, and the icing comes out of the bag in the shape of the mold. Two things are necessary: the mold and pressure.

This is the picture the Bible presents of what happens to us in the world. We are put under pressure from every side to be "conformed," to be squeezed into destructive ways of thinking and living. Some of these destructive ways of thinking into which we are molded are listed below. As you read these ways of thinking, put a check mark by any that you can identify as having become a part of your thinking.

Codependent thinking—A compulsion to control and rescue people by fixing their problems, even if they don't ask for it. This is from the codependent's need for self-worth.

Compulsive behavior thinking—A driving impulse to act on something without considering your choices and/or consequences.

Controlling thinking—An attempt to exercise restraint or control over someone. You communicate things like, "If you'll just do this right, then I'll love you/accept you/approve of you."

Addictive thinking—The thought that "it" (whatever "it" is) will fix me.

Approval thinking—If I just do what "they" (whoever "they" are) say, then I will be O.K. (a good person, an acceptable person, etc.)

Low self-image thinking—No matter what I do or what people tell me, I know I am not worthy.

What are some other ways of thinking, into which you might have been squeezed, that have become destructive in your life?

____

____

____

____

____

b. Be transformed by the renewing of your mind

God's purpose for us is that we be transformed from the way of thinking that we have been squeezed into by the world. The word "transformed" is one of the most descriptive, beautiful, and encouraging words in the entire Bible. It assures us that real and lasting change can take place in our lives. The word in the original language of the New Testament (Greek) is *metamorphoomai*. We derive our biological term "metamorphosis" from this word. It's the word that is used to describe the change that takes place as a caterpillar weaves a cocoon, and with time, emerges as a beautiful butterfly. In the cocoon, a "transformation" takes place that we call "metamorphosis."

This is the work that God desires to do in our lives. Transformation from the caterpillar to the butterfly. How does He do this work? When we "present our bodies"—turn ownership over to Him, turn our will and the care of our lives over to Him—He begins to "renew" our minds! Every action is preceded by a thought. The way we think determines the way we act. If our behavior is destructive, it is because first, our thinking is destructive. The world wants to squeeze us into a mold of destructive thinking that leads into destructive behavior. This is part of Satan's strategy to defeat God's good purpose in our lives. The loving heavenly Father wants to renew our thinking into right, healthy thinking, so the result will be right, healthy behavior!

Here are some examples of how this process works. If you believe or think you are not a person of worth and value (low self-esteem thinking), then your behavior will reflect that belief. If you believe that you must be in control to be secure (controlling thinking), then your behavior will be controlling behavior. If you believe you need a chemical crutch to be happy (addictive thinking), your behavior will reflect that thinking. If you believe you are only validated as a person when you are in a relationship (codependent thinking), then you will move from destructive relationship to destructive relationship, seeking to validate yourself. For those behaviors to change from destructive to constructive, the thinking behind the behaviors must first change. God wants to renew your mind.

The process of growth requires patience and perseverance, as opposed to expecting change to happen immediately. We didn't get to the place we are now overnight, and God's work of changing our destructive thinking won't happen overnight. How do you feel about that?

____

____

____

____

____

3. Transformation Leads to a Revelation

When you "present your body" (turn over control and ownership to Him), and cease to be "conformed" to the world, but rather allow Him to "transform you by the renewing of your mind," then you begin to experience the will of God which is "good, acceptable and perfect."

What is the will of God for you? Jesus said it in John 10:10:

> *"The thief [Enemy] comes only to steal, kill, and destroy; I came that they may have life, and have it abundantly."*

This is His will for you. He wants you to have life to its fullest. That is the will of God which is "good and acceptable and perfect." The old faulty patterns of thinking that led to faulty patterns of living didn't bring you abundant life. Abundance is possible only if you allow God to renew your mind.

God has given each of us the ability to choose. When we submit ourselves to our addictions or compulsions, we are making a choice to give control over to another source. Our freedom to choose brings with it the responsibility for our choices. We experience the consequences of our choices. If you have come to realize that your life, at least in some areas, needs to change, and you have not been able to bring about this change yourself, then a decision is required. A decision to present your body turns your will and the care of your life over to God.

If you are interested in finding out how to present your body through placing your faith in Jesus Christ and beginning the process of renewing of your mind, then read about the pathway to Christ that follows. Two things are important to understand about presenting your body. It happens at a point in time and then continues as a process. The point in time is when you receive Christ as Savior. The continuing process is deciding every day to submit your will to Him that day.

The Point of Surrender

Salvation through Christ

1. God—The Bible Says That

a. God is ______________________________

We have come to know and have believed the love which God has for us. God is love, and the one who abides in love abides in God, and God abides in him. (1 John 4:16)

He loves His creation and all that is in it. This means He loves and cares for you. The question isn't, "Does God love me?" The question is, "Will I experience God's love in my life?" That is dependent upon my choice.

b. God is ______________________________

But like the Holy One who called you, be holy yourselves also in all your behavior; because it is written, "You shall be Holy for I am Holy." (1 Peter 1:15-16)

To be holy means to be separate from sin. God is completely separate from sin. Because He is holy, He cannot dwell in the presence of sin. This is why the Bible says that the "condition" of sin outside of Christ separates us from God.

c. God is ______________________________

For I proclaim the name of the Lord; ascribe greatness to our God! The Rock!

His work is perfect, For all His ways are just; A God of faithfulness and without injustice, Righteous and upright is He. (Deuteronomy 32:3–4)

God's justice means He always deals fairly. He never says one thing and does another. Also, He must do what He says.

2. People—The Bible Says That

a. People are ________________________________

For all have sinned and fall short of the glory of God. (Romans 3:23)

This doesn't mean everything people do is bad. That certainly is not true. It means mankind has a fallen nature that we inherited from our spiritual parents, Adam and Eve. It means we have a tendency toward self-will and rebellion against God's will and plan. That self-will has tainted every area of our lives and separated us from God.

Have you experienced this truth in the behavior of others toward you in your life? How?

____

____

____

____

Have you demonstrated this truth in your life? How?

____

____

____

____

b. People have the sentence of ________________________________

For the wages of sin is death, but the free gift of God is eternal life in Christ Jesus our Lord. (Romans 6:23)

At this point, we need to stop and review what we have learned. God loves His creation. He created us so that He might express His love. He created us in perfection just as He is perfect. There was no death, no sickness, and no sin. Therefore, mankind had perfect access and an unhindered relationship to his perfect and holy Creator. God told man and woman that as long as they chose obedience to His will, they would have life. But the result of rebellion against His will would be death.

The Lord God commanded the man, saying, "From any tree of the garden you may eat freely; but from the tree of the knowledge of good and evil you shall not eat, for in the day that you eat from it you will surely die." (Genesis 2:16-17)

The death that is spoken of in Genesis 2:17 is not only physical death, but also spiritual death, which means separation from God. God had to exclude mankind from His presence because of His holiness. He cannot dwell in the presence of unholiness. His justice required that He do what He said He would do! Mankind had to die because that is what God told man would happen! But God is also love and He created mankind to express His love. So what He did was provide a way by which mankind, who is imperfect and sinful, could return to a relationship with Him who is perfect and holy. That is what He did in Jesus Christ.

3. Christ—The Bible Says That

a. Christ ____

But God demonstrates His own love toward us, in that while we were yet sinners, Christ died for us. (Romans 5:8)

When it says He died "for" us, it means He died "in our place." He took our sentence for us. He satisfied the justice of God that demanded the sentence of death be carried out, by taking that sentence upon Himself. What qualified Christ to do this?

b. He lived a ______________________________________ life.

And having been made perfect, He became to all those who obey Him the source of eternal salvation. (Hebrews 5:9)

A perfect God requires a perfect sacrifice. Christ was born without a human father and therefore without the "sin nature" that all the rest of us of are born with. In other words, He was born the same way Adam was created—perfect, without sin. Where Adam chose to sin, Jesus chose to perfectly obey the Father.

c. He laid that perfect life down as a perfect ______________________

And walk in love, just as Christ also loved you and gave Himself up for us, an offering and a sacrifice to God . . . (Ephesians 5:2)

Since God is a perfect God, the only kind of sacrifice that would be sufficient is a perfect sacrifice of a sinless life. Jesus lived that life and made that sacrifice.

d. God raised Jesus from the ______________________

"Let it be known to all of you and to all the people of Israel, that by the name of Jesus Christ the Nazarene, whom you crucified, whom God raised from the dead—by this name this man stands here before you in good health." (Acts 4:10)

This is the significance of the resurrection of Jesus: By raising Christ from the dead, God was saying, "I accept that sacrifice. It is good enough to pay the price; to satisfy my justice." This is why Jesus could say,

"I am the way, and the truth, and the life; no one comes to the Father but through Me." (John 14:6)

This brings us to the last person. Ourselves. What must we do to have His sacrifice applied to us?

4. You—The Bible Says That

a. What you must do. ______________________ Christ as Savior.

But as many as received Him, to them He gave the right to become children of God . . . (John 1:12a)

How do you receive Christ?

b. Receive Him by ______________________

For by grace you have been saved . . . (Ephesians 2:8a)

By definition, "grace" means something that is unearned and undeserved. Grace, in other words, means as a gift. Salvation isn't something that anyone can earn. If we were going to earn a right relationship with God, we would have to be perfect because He is perfect. We can't be perfect, but Jesus is. So, we must be willing to receive salvation not as an act of our own works, but as a free gift of God based upon the perfect sacrifice of Jesus. How do we receive this free gift?

c. Receive Him through ______________________________

For by grace you have been saved through faith; and that is not of yourselves, it is the gift of God; not as a result of works, so that no one may boast. (Ephesians 2:8-9)

At this point, it is important to understand the meaning of faith. Faith is a commitment. Faith is an action. In the earlier illustration about the guy and the wheelbarrow, faith isn't standing there saying we believe the guy could carry us across. Those are just words. It would be faith when we got in the wheelbarrow. Saying we *believe* that Jesus Christ died on the cross for our sins isn't faith. Faith is when we commit our life to Him because we know He died on the cross for our sins.

5. What You Receive

a. Forgiveness

If we confess our sins, He is faithful and righteous to forgive us our sins and to cleanse us from all unrighteousness. (1 John 1:9)

b. New potential for this life

Therefore if anyone is in Christ, he is a new creature; the old things passed away; behold, new things have come. (2 Corinthians 5:17)

c. The promise of eternal life

And the testimony is this, that God has given us eternal life, and this life is in His Son. He who has the Son has the life; he who does not have the Son of God does not have the life. (1 John 5:11–12)

6. How You Receive Christ

Receiving Christ is a matter of the heart, not the words. This is a simple prayer that you can pray to receive Christ's forgiveness and new life. Remember, these are not magical words. If these words do not reflect the attitude of your heart, they are empty and meaningless. But, if this is the attitude of your heart, He knows and has promised to come into your life and give you salvation.

Lord Jesus, I admit I am powerless to save myself. I believe that you died on the cross for my sin. I now act on that belief by surrendering my life and my will to you. I accept your death on the cross as payment for my sins. Thank you for forgiving me and giving me a new life. Thank you for the new life that is now mine through you. Please help me to grow in my understanding of your love and power so that my life will bring glory and honor to you. In Jesus' name I pray, Amen.

There is nothing magical about these specific words. God looks beyond the words anyway and looks into the heart. These words simply reflect the attitude of the heart that is necessary to receive Christ as Savior.

What are you feeling right now? Fear, doubt, excitement? Why?

____

____

____

____

If you have already made the commitment of your life to Christ and know for certain that Christ is in your life, write down when that happened.

____

____

____

____

If you are ready to make the commitment of your life to Christ, you can do it right now where you are. Simply tell that to God and sincerely mean it in your heart. If you do, then sign and date your signature as a reminder of the moment that you received new life in Christ.

Signature: ______________________________________

Date: ____________________

Perhaps you are not ready to make this commitment of your life to Christ. Please know that we understand. We were all at that point at one time in our own lives. Everyone must make this decision on their own when they are fully ready. Anything else would not be genuine. Perhaps something that would help you would be to perform an experiment. For the next 30 days, ask God every day to reveal to you the truth of who Jesus Christ is and your need for Him. Over those days, review the Scriptures you have read above and look at the changed lives of Christians in your freedom group. If you are genuinely open to God, we believe He will guide you.

If you are willing to perform this 30-day prayer experiment, sign your name and date your signature.

Signature: ____________________

Date: ____________________

7. *The Process of Surrender*

Surrender daily to Christ

Salvation comes at the point when you surrender yourself to Christ as Savior. Then the rest of life is about the daily decision to surrender your will for that day. In the Bible, this is called "sanctification." It refers to the continual process of allowing Christ to lead you, direct you and change you. The apostle Paul spoke about both of these types of surrender.

> *I have been crucified with Christ; and it is no longer I who live, but Christ lives in me; and the life which I now live in the flesh I live by faith in the Son of God, who loved me and gave Himself up for me. (Galatians 2:20)*

In this passage, he spoke about the point of surrender when he came to know Christ. He uses the image of being crucified with Christ. He died to himself and his will. But then there is that daily decision that each of us must make to crucify our own will and desires so that His will and desires can be realized in our lives.

> *I affirm, brethren, by the boasting in you which I have in Christ Jesus our Lord, I die daily. (1 Corinthians 15:31)*

Often, Christians are confused about what it means to "die daily." What can I do to surrender my will and the care of my life daily to God? The answer is found in practicing the principles that you will discover in Steps D through J. These steps will give you a plan and some tools to help you to "die daily." They will also give you evidence that you have really come to the point of truly accepting Christ as Savior.

If you decide not to take this step of the journey, what is your alternative?

What is the single most significant thing you have learned in this step?

What do you intend to do in your marriage this week as a result of this step?

TABLE TALK

What is the most important thing about you that relates to this chapter, that you are going to share with your spouse this week?

JOURNAL

8

"D"—Discover Responsibility

"Made a searching and fearless moral inventory of ourselves."

THE PROBLEM OF "D"

The problem this step presents may be the greatest challenge we will face in this process. In this step, we will be challenged to take a "fearless and searching moral inventory." Rigorous honesty is required to take this inventory and rigorous honesty is never an easy thing to achieve.

One of the most detested, yet necessary, tasks any business owner must perform is the inventory of goods. However, aside from the fact that the tax man requires it, there are other valid reasons to do the inventory. The first reason is to discover how many of certain goods are still in stock. Taking inventory lets the businessperson know what goods are selling and what goods need to be restocked so that more can be sold. That is a beneficial purpose of taking an inventory.

The second reason for the inventory is so the business owner can discover items that are not selling and need to be liquidated. Those items have become a liability because they are tying up valuable storage space and resources that could be utilized for purchasing and inventorying items that will sell. The purpose of business is to sell stuff! If stuff isn't selling, then it isn't working for the business but is working against the business.

The process of taking a fearless and searching moral inventory also has both positive and negative aspects. By taking an inventory, we identify those good qualities that need to be recognized, celebrated, and built upon. That is the enjoyable part. The other part is more difficult. We have to identify those things that are a liability to us. Those things that are draining our valuable emotional and spiritual resources away. As we go through this process, we have to look into the deepest, darkest corners of our lives and go into those places where dust and debris have built up. Identifying and ultimately becoming willing to get rid of those resource-robbing and energy-draining attitudes, thoughts, and behaviors is not easy. However, when we complete it, we will find that much more space is made available to us for the good that is already there to be enlarged, and room is created for the new thoughts, habits, attitudes, and actions that will bring positive results in our lives.

The downside to the inventory, and the reason many drop out of the process at this point, is that the process can be painful. Nobody likes it. It's meticulous. It can be humiliating and even scary to face some of what is really tucked away on those back shelves of our lives and hearts. You could say that this discovery part of the process is the "Death Valley" of the journey. Halfway across the valley, we begin to think there is no way we can go all the way across. It's hot, dry, desolate, and we fear we will die right there in the valley. But on the other side are the beautiful mountains where it's cool, there is plenty of water, and the scenery is beautiful. You have to cross the valley to get to the mountains. We encourage you to go the distance. Cross the valley so we can climb the mountains on the other side together.

THE PROCESS OF "D"

One way of illustrating what we are doing in this step is to think of a giant cruise ship. The ship is maintained immaculately above the water line. It is painted regularly; the deck and woodwork shines, the chrome sparkles, and the engines are kept in tip-top shape. However, because the hull is beneath the water line and is not visible, it is never touched. Over time, as the ship sits in the ocean, barnacles begin to attach themselves to the hull. At first, it isn't that much of a problem because the ship has powerful engines to drive it through the water. But as the years go by, more and more barnacles attach themselves to the hull. Eventually, so much drag on the ship is created by the barnacles that it can barely move through the water. Everything above the water line still looks good. The engines are still working to full capacity and everything still sparkles above the water line. However, what is beneath the water line is keeping the ship from functioning as it was built to function. Our lives are much like this ship. It's the things hidden beneath the water line that cause the most detriment in our lives. We work very diligently to keep what is above the water line in shape, but all of this is negated if we don't do some below-the-water-line maintenance.

In the fourth step, we are going to put on our scuba gear, go beneath the water line, and scrape the barnacles from the hull of our ship. The moral inventory is intended to help us quit treating the symptoms and get to the cause. Our purpose is to discover the barnacles of attitudes and behaviors that have created unhealthy results in our lives. When we discover them, we can begin to look at them objectively and decide on new ways of thinking and new patterns of behavior. This is the "renewing of the mind" that Scripture speaks about.

Of necessity, taking this inventory will involve thinking about our family of origin. For each of us, our family of origin has had a profound influence on who we are today, in both positive and negative ways. There are two extremes that we must avoid at this point. The first extreme is to pretend our family of origin was perfect. They weren't perfect; no family is. To look honestly at our family and admit any negative effects it might have had on us is not a betrayal of the family. It is simply an admission of fact.

Many of our families were doing the best they could with what they had been given by their family of origin. Somewhere, the chain must be broken, and this requires that we look honestly and openly at our family. If we are unwilling to do this, we will likely be condemned to repeat those mistakes generation after generation.

The other extreme is to use our family of origin as an excuse for the continuation of our own irresponsible choices and actions. The truth is, regardless of what set the stage for our problems, we must now take responsibility for what we choose to do about it. Blaming our family of origin won't bring release from the things that hold us in bondage. It will only reinforce and strengthen the chains that hold us. Take a few moments and think about your family of origin.

In a sentence, see if you can sum up your family of origin.

____

____

____

____

____

What was your role in the family (peacekeeper, hero, black sheep, etc.)?

____

____

____

____

____

What role did others play (father, mother, siblings)?

____

____

____

____

How did you feel about your role in the family?

____

____

____

____

What effects has your family of origin had on your adult life (anger, resentment, rebellion, bitterness, etc.)?

____

____

____

____

The second thing we have to do is look honestly at the hurtful experiences we have suffered in life. Sometimes these hurts are the result of our own bad choices. Sometimes they are the result of choices others have made and those choices have affected us negatively. All of these things inform and mold our minds, thoughts, attitudes, and behaviors.

Let me say again, however, that in looking at our past experiences and families of origin we are not looking for excuses, but explanations. Many of us have made excuses all our lives for our attitudes and actions. As long as we are making excuses, we will never experience change. Our purpose is to look for explanations for why we struggle in certain thought patterns, attitudes, and behaviors, and from there we can then experience change. This step in the process is about discovering our responsibility and taking full responsibility for our thoughts, beliefs, attitudes, and actions.

It is helpful for us to understand how these things have happened within us. In other words, to discover explanations for our tendencies. However, we must never see these explanations as excuses.

This concept is sometimes difficult to understand. Therefore, we need to spend some time looking at it in more depth so we can be certain that we have achieved understanding. First, it will be helpful to understand the difference between circumstances and consequences.

Circumstances

Circumstances are things over which we have no control or input. For instance, the family into which I was born is a circumstance. I had no control or input into that event. Also, many things that happen to us when we are children are circumstances. Child abuse in all of its forms is a circumstance. Abandonment is a circumstance. In adulthood, the loss of a job due to corporate downsizing or outsourcing can be a circumstance. It may have nothing to do with my job performance. It's the result of forces that are beyond my control and into which I had no input.

Think for a moment of some circumstances that have happened in your life.

1. ______________________________

2. ______________________________

3. ______________________________

4. ______________________________

5. ______________________________

Consequences

Consequences are pretty much everything else that happens in my life. Consequences are the result of choices I have made. I have come to believe that life is, at most, 10 percent circumstances and about 90 percent consequences. This gives me great encouragement for change because, unlike circumstances, I do have control over consequences. I can control consequences by my choices. This is because consequences are purely the result of the choices I have made. Choices bring consequences. I have heard it said, "We make our choices and then our choices make us." Another way of saying it is, "Our lives are the sum total of the choices that we have made." That includes both choices I make before circumstances and choices I make after circumstances happen.

Think for a moment about things in your life that are consequences—the result of choices you have made. (Look above at what you said were circumstances. Do you need to rethink any of those now?)

1. ______________________________

2. ______________________________

3. ______________________________

4. ______________________________

5. ______________________________

Sometimes it can be very difficult for us initially to make the distinction. Often, upon close examination, we find that things we once thought were circumstances were actually consequences. Sometimes circumstances are preceded by choices that we have to take responsibility for, even though we had no control over the circumstance. This is difficult, but it is work that must be done because this step is about discovering personal responsibility. If I am going to make this discovery, I must first understand what I am responsible for and what I am not responsible for.

The Scripture clearly teaches that choices bring consequences. It is how God has designed creation to work.

> *Do not be deceived, God is not mocked; for whatever a man sows, this he will also reap. (Galatians 6:7)*

In fact, when God's Old Testament people, the Hebrew nation, first entered into the Promised Land, He told them it was His choice to give them the land. How they lived in the land would be the result of choices they would have to make.

> *See, I am setting before you today a blessing and a curse; the blessing, if you listen to the commandments of the Lord your God, which I am commanding you today; and the curse, if you do not listen to the commandments of the Lord your God, but turn aside from the way which I am commanding you today, by following other gods which you have not known. (Deuteronomy 11:26–28)*

Jesus basically said the same thing. Eternal life is a promise from God, given as a gift when we place our faith in Christ as Savior (like the Promised Land was for the Hebrews). However, abundant life while here on earth (John 10:10) is not a promise, but only a potential that He makes available to us. Whether we live in this potential or not is determined by the choices we make. If we choose to honor Him and obey Him, we move into abundant life (the blessing). If we choose not to honor Him and obey Him, we harvest the consequences of those choices (the curse).

To help you understand this distinction, I have developed the illustration below. We will refer to it in the discussion that follows.

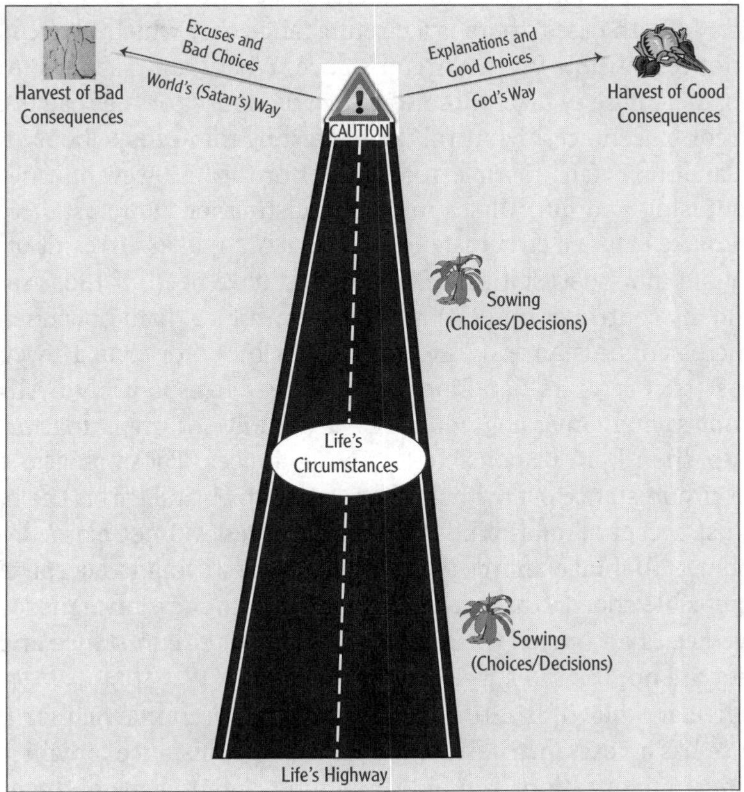

Let's begin with circumstances on the chart. Circumstances happen over which I have no control or input. It can be anything that fits that definition. However, immediately after the circumstance, I am faced with choices. I choose how I am going to respond to that circumstance. As I make these choices and these decisions, I have moved onto life's highway, and I am planting seeds that are going to bring a harvest. These choices can go in one of two directions. This is where the caution sign comes in. This is a critical fork in the road and the fork that I choose will determine what consequences I harvest in my life. If I choose to see the circumstance as an excuse for anger, bitterness, resentment, or unforgiveness, then those are the seeds that will be planted in my life. Those seeds will eventually bring a crop—a harvest in my life. As Galatians 6:7 says, this harvest will be identical in nature to the seed I have planted. Therefore, I am responsible for this crop. It's the result of my own choices, not the circumstance! The circumstance didn't cause these consequences. My choices did.

If I choose to see my circumstance not as an excuse but as an explanation of why, perhaps, I struggle in certain areas or deal with certain feelings, then I can choose to make good choices that honor God and others, and the result will be a harvest of good consequences. In both cases, there is a circumstance over which I have no control or input. I am not responsible for the circumstance. What I am responsible for is which fork in the road I choose to take. Either the road of excuses or the road of explanation. Good choices or bad choices. I control the harvest by the seeds I choose to plant.

This explanation is fairly simple and straightforward. However, sometimes, it can get more confusing and difficult to make the distinction. For instance, sometimes the choices I make before a circumstance happens can make the result of the circumstance in my life more devastating than it should have been. If I lose my job due to things beyond my control or input, that is a circumstance. I am now unemployed and this is a difficult circumstance. I have no responsibility for that. However, if I have spent the past twenty years handling my resources irresponsibly by living beyond my means, not saving, amassing consumer debt, and not preparing for unexpected circumstances, then I am responsible for those choices. Those choices increase the effects of the circumstance over which I have no control, and this is the harvest of my choices. I must accept responsibility for those choices and not blame everything on the circumstance. As I take an inventory, I have to be willing to accept responsibility for my irresponsible choices that are now making my circumstance more critical than it would have been had I made wiser choices. The two, circumstance and choice, are connected but are not the same.

Let me give another illustration. Suppose I have been married for twenty years and my spouse has an extramarital affair. That is a circumstance for which there is no excuse, justification, or rationalization. It is wrong, and it is one of the most extreme acts of betrayal and violation of trust that a human being can experience. The wounds from the betrayal are deep and very hurtful. Without negating the culpability of my spouse for his/her act of betrayal, if I am going to be honest in my inventory, I must try to discover if there is anything I need to take responsibility for in the marriage. For instance, was I attentive to my spouse's needs? Was I distant emotionally? Did I neglect my spouse with my pursuit of work, career, or recreation? Was I abusive verbally, sexually, or physically in any way? You get the idea. None of those things excuse the act of infidelity. That was a choice the spouse made, and he/she will have to be responsible for that choice. What I have to do is take responsibility for what I did or didn't do in the marriage.

Not only that, but I have to look at the choices I have made since the infidelity. Did I see my spouse's act as an excuse to go out and have my own affair as payback? If I did, I made that choice. My spouse's infidelity didn't force me to do it. He or she didn't put a gun to my head and force me to do it. There is no excuse for my behavior. I made the choice, and I am responsible for that choice. I took the fork in the road of seeing the circumstance as an excuse and that led me to make a bad choice. Have I allowed bitterness and anger and cynicism to invade my heart since my spouse's infidelity? Others might tell me it's natural and understandable for me to do that. Maybe it is from the world's perspective, but what good is this going to do for me? None! Those attitudes will infect every relationship I enter into until I recognize them and release them from my heart. In other words, the choices I am now making are planting bad seeds that are going to bring a bad harvest in my inner spirit and relationships.

In Hebrews 12:15, we are warned not to allow any "root of bitterness" to spring up because it "causes trouble, and by it many are defiled." The problem with bitterness is, it defiles me! It doesn't stay compartmentalized only toward the person against whom I harbor it. It defiles me, and therefore I carry that defilement into every relationship I have in my life. With God, others, and myself. The seed of bitterness (that I choose to plant) will bring a negative harvest (consequence) in my life.

What I must do now is choose to see the circumstance of my spouse's infidelity only as an explanation, not an excuse. It explains why I am now struggling with these negative responses, but it doesn't excuse them! I must choose not to entertain those negative choices anymore; and if I have in the past, I must be willing to admit that and accept responsibility for my own choices when taking my personal inventory. The purpose for this rigorous honesty is not to beat myself up with guilt or shame. Its purpose is to admit the truth and my responsibility for my own choices (which is all I have any control over), so I can move beyond them and begin to make good choices that will bring good consequences in the future.

Therefore, in taking a rigorously honest inventory, I must ask myself two questions in every circumstance.

1. What are the choices that I made after that circumstance for which I must take full responsibility?

2. What are the choices that I made leading up to that circumstance (if any) for which I must now take full responsibility?

Like Peeling Fruit

Dealing with choices is a lot like peeling an apple. You have to peel away the skin and even deeper to get to the core. In this illustration the core is my attitudes and actions and the consequences they have brought. The skin and everything else that surrounds the core are circumstances. If I never get beneath the circumstances I can never get to the core. It is at the core where I really get honest and admit my responsibility. This is when change becomes possible.

This is a fearless and searching moral inventory. This is the kind of rigorous honesty that will enable me to clear out the destructive attitudes, beliefs, and behaviors, that have brought nothing good in my life, and replace them with choices that will bring good things into my life.

Let me say it again, if I am going to make changes, I must first discover the things I am responsible for, accept that responsibility, then move beyond those choices into new and better choices. I must stop making excuses and blaming circumstances or others for the negative things happening in my life, and begin to look for explanations and solutions.

Of course, if you are happy with the consequences (harvest) you are getting in your life, then keep on planting those same seeds. However, if you do not like the harvest, you must plant different seeds. New and better choices (seeds) bring new and better consequences (harvest) in my life in my relationship to God, others, and myself. Ask yourself the question, "How's it workin' out for me?" If you don't like how it's working out for you, then you need to address the problem of the choices you are making.

Hope in the Harvest

During this process we have to be careful that hopelessness does not overwhelm us. Sometimes, when we become aware that so much that has happened in our lives, and may be continuing to happen, is the harvest of our choices, we can move into despair, hopelessness, and self-condemnation. However, this is a time we need to be reminded that God is sovereign over even our bad choices! That doesn't mean he caused them but rather He can use even these things we are harvesting in our lives to bring good. This is the testimony of the Scripture.

> *And we know that God causes all things to work together for good to those who love God, to those who are called according to His purpose. (Romans 8:28)*

What an encouragement that verse is. Rather than allowing the harvest to destroy any hope of a better life, I can turn these consequences over to God, accept that the harvest is going to come in, and know that if I look to Him He will bring good out of those consequences in my life. There are things He wants to teach me in the midst of the harvest. If I listen to Him, learn from Him, and obey Him, then He will turn even the struggle into good in my life.

Not only that, but if God doesn't condemn us, then we shouldn't condemn ourselves. The testimony of Scripture is that Christ took our condemnation for all our sins and failures. There is no condemnation left for us to take when we are in Christ.

Therefore there is now no condemnation for those who are in Christ Jesus. (Romans 8:1)

In fact, I want you to keep reminding yourself of this truth as you work through this difficult process. Every time you begin to feel overwhelmed with shame, guilt, or self-condemnation, remind yourself of this truth.

Truth: If you are in the process the heavenly Father is pleased!

What harvest is there in your life right now out of which you can see a possibility for God to bring good?

____

____

____

Tools for the Inventory

To do the process of discovery, it would be helpful to have a guide. Traditionally, people who are involved in twelve-step groups have used a list known as the "Seven Deadly Sins" as a guide for doing the moral inventory. This list did not originate with the twelve steps. It has its roots as far back as the sixth century! This means the list is pretty old, but still very applicable. And, it actually goes further back than that! All of these "deadlies" are issues the Scriptures address. God's Word was the first to shine the spotlight on these attitudes and actions. The basic things humans struggle with haven't changed very much through the centuries, so this list is as current as today's newspaper. Allow me to give a quick overview of the seven deadlies, and then you can use them as a catalyst to inventory your own struggle.

The Seven Deadly Sins

1. Pride

Pride goes before destruction, and a haughty spirit before stumbling. (Proverbs 16:18)

It shouldn't be any surprise that pride is the first on the list. It's the primary character defect of mankind. It is the most basic of all sins. For some, pride will even keep them from completing this fourth step. It's pride that causes us to want to rationalize and justify our actions. It's pride that makes us want to control others around us. It's pride that keeps us from wanting to admit our problems and being willing to deal with them.

2. Anger

Do not be eager in your heart to be angry, for anger resides in the bosom [heart] of fools. (Ecclesiastes 7:9)

When the Bible speaks of anger, it usually is talking about the toxic, stored-up kind. Some expressions of anger are not wrong and may even be the most appropriate response to a given situation, such as injustice, or cruelty to the defenseless. But this kind of anger goes away when the situation is over. The anger that is destructive is that which is stored away for the long term. It's the anger that comes from being deeply hurt by other people or by circumstances in life. The Bible says it resides in the heart of fools because this kind of anger leads us to do stupid, self-destructive kinds of things.

3. Greed

He who profits illicitly troubles his own house, but he who hates bribes will live. (Proverbs 15:27)

What is it that drives us to have more and more, even at the expense of relationships, integrity, and character, and keep more and more of it for ourselves? Greed. Greed drives much of what we do in western culture and is the root of a great deal of harm that we do to ourselves and to others around us.

4. Lust

"But I say to you everyone who looks at a woman with lust for her has already committed adultery with her in his heart." (Matthew 5:28)

Lust is a matter of the heart. Lust is the natural God-given sexual drive allowed to run amuck! It is a way of mentally reducing another person to an object to be used and played with for one's own selfish pleasure.

5. Envy

Let us not become boastful, challenging one another, envying one another. (Galatians 5:26)

Shakespeare called envy the "green sickness." Envy causes us to obsess over someone else and what they have. It is the source of jealousy, competitiveness, and all kinds of destructive behavior. Envy poisons life because it poisons relationships.

6. Gluttony

For the heavy drinker and the glutton will come to poverty. (Proverbs 23:21)

Gluttony is most often associated with overeating, but it can relate to anything we do in excess. Gluttony, in any form, is a means of attempting to compensate for internal pain by over-indulgence. When related to food particularly, it leads to other deep issues such as shattered self-esteem, shaming, and severe health risks.

7. Sloth

I passed by the field of the sluggard and by the vineyard of the man lacking sense, And behold it was completely overgrown with thistles; its surface was covered with nettles, and its stone wall was broken down. (Proverbs 24:30–31)

Sloth is simply laziness! Sloth and laziness may not be a problem in every area of life. We may work hard at our job or our career but neglect our marriage or children by not putting in the time that they need.

When we look at the seven deadly sins, it's a pretty bleak and scary picture that we see. It's difficult for any of us to admit that these kinds of things are operating in our lives. Our tendency is to begin to draw back and return to denial, rationalization, and justification. The Bible tells us that our heart has a tendency to deceive us. This is one of the reasons change happens best in the context of community. Often, we are only able to see ourselves as others share their struggles and problems. In other words, the Holy Spirit shines the light of truth upon my heart, which can deceive me, through the understanding others have gained about themselves.

The heart is more deceitful than all else and is desperately sick; Who can understand it? "I, the Lord, search the heart, I test the mind, Even to give to each man according to his ways." (Jeremiah 17:9–10)

The Fruit of the Spirit

But the fruit of the Spirit is love, joy, peace, patience, kindness, goodness, faithfulness, gentleness, self-control; against such things there is no law. (Galatians 5:22–23)

Attitudes are often very difficult for us to identify. This is primarily because they aren't as visible as actions are. It's simple to see an action and put a name to it. However, since our attitudes are internal, it is sometimes difficult for us to recognize the destructive attitude and put a name to it. Therefore, I want to give you another diagnostic tool to help you put a name to attitudes. The tool is the list of the nine characteristics of "the fruit of the Spirit."

The fruit of the Spirit is what the Spirit of God wants to create within us. Their source is in the Spirit. Notice, they aren't really actions, but rather attitudes. The actions God desires flow out of these attitudes. This list of fruit, along with their opposites, is a tool we can use to diagnose our attitudes. Use this list, along with the seven deadlies, to help you diagnose your attitudes.

Fruit of the Spirit	Opposite of the Fruit of the Spirit
1. Love	Bitterness, resentment, hatred
2. Joy	Negativism, self-loathing
3. Peace	Anxiety, inner conflict
4. Patience	Dissatisfaction, irritability
5. Kindness	Suspicion, uncaring
6. Goodness	Defensiveness, selfishness
7. Faithfulness	Self-centered, noncommittal
8. Gentleness	Anger, rage, aggression
9. Self-control	Self-indulgence

Can you point to an attitude or behavior that reminds you that you have a deceitful heart?

____

____

____

What fears or anxieties do you have about delving into memories of your past in order to take this inventory?

____

____

____

An Understanding of Attitudes and Actions

The purpose of the moral inventory is not just to remember things we have done wrong in the past, but also to understand why we did them. We want to understand the underlying reasons. In the moral inventory, we will focus on attitudes and actions.

Hurt first produces a destructive attitude. Destructive actions most often follow on the heels of the destructive attitude. Therefore, we don't want to focus on the action alone, but to identify and address the attitude out of which the action was born. Both of these are vital to an effective and life-changing moral inventory. Most of our destructive attitudes can be boiled down to three sources. However, almost all of our destructive attitudes spring from one key source: anger. Anger expresses itself in many ways and can result from many kinds of experiences. However, usually anger is at the root of destructive attitudes and actions. The following discussion identifies three sources of anger and, thus, destructive attitudes.

1. Hurt

When we are hurt we can become angry. If you attempt to help a wounded animal, the animal will often strike out at you because it is hurt. If you hit your finger with a hammer, you have a flash of anger. That kind of anger is short-lived and isn't destructive. The kind of anger that is destructive results from deeper hurts that are the result of emotional wounds. These deep hurts are most often received in childhood or early adolescence when we are the most vulnerable. They may result from physical abuse, emotional abuse, abandonment, or just not having basic needs met for security and affection.

What hurts can you identify that may have negatively affected your life?

____

____

____

2. Frustration

When we are frustrated, we often become angry. We have all seen a child playing with a shape sorter, trying to hammer that square peg into a round hole. After awhile, he starts screaming and throwing pieces all over the room. He has become frustrated, which has resulted in anger. Sometimes the anger that we feel is the result of the frustrations of life. Maybe there have been unrealized dreams or unfulfilled goals. Maybe we have perceived failures in our lives. Maybe we sit down and look at our life and it just hasn't turned out the way we had envisioned. Perhaps there is frustration and, beneath that, anger.

What kinds of frustrations do you have in your life that have resulted in anger?

---

3. Fears

Fear is often the root of anger. We have a temporary fear mechanism that is God-given and is there for our protection. It's called the fight-or-flight syndrome. When we are suddenly frightened, a shot of adrenalin goes into the bloodstream, heart rate goes up, respiration goes up, we become angry at the threat and are able to respond by defending ourselves. When the threat is gone, the body returns to normal and the anger is gone. However, sustained fear and anxiety can have devastating results on us physically and emotionally. When events in life have resulted in a continuous state of anxiety or fear, the body is never able to relax, the anger level stays constant and life begins to spiral out of control.

What kinds of fears or anxieties are there in your life? Can you identify where they came from?

Guidelines for the Inventory

Only a few more preparations and we will be ready to begin our moral inventory. Several guidelines need to be mentioned that will help you get the most benefit out of this process.

1. Write it down.

The following pages are provided for you to write down your thoughts. Writing them down is helpful because seeing things in writing makes them more concrete. Also, you will be able to identify patterns of behavior.

2. Keep a pen and paper with you 24 hours a day during this process.

While you are out and around at work or driving down the road, God will bring situations to your mind. You need a way to write them down when they come to your mind. Then, when you are back at your workbook, you can develop them more fully.

3. Ask daily for God's revelations to you.

Ask Him to show you things and bring things to your memory that perhaps you would never think of or remember otherwise. When they come, thank Him for answering your prayer.

4. Remember you will not be required to discuss this with the group.

This is for your own personal good and you will share only what you wish to share with the group. This inventory will give you a framework for completing later steps, but you will never be forced to share with the group anything that you are not ready to share. So, be honest and write everything down, no matter how repulsive it may be to you at the time.

Explanation of the Inventory Worksheets

I have seen moral inventory processes that were so complicated it would be difficult to imagine how anyone could understand how to complete the work. Therefore, I have attempted to make this as simple as possible. Two examples follow; the first is of a completed General Life Inventory Worksheet and the second a completed Marriage Inventory Worksheet.

Example of Completed General Life Inventory Worksheet:

1. What happened and who was involved?

My boss treats me like I am stupid. He doesn't treat me with respect. Maybe it isn't a current boss, but one from years before. Maybe it is several bosses! List them one by one as separate circumstances.

2. My attitude before:

I was unfriendly. Reclusive. Non-engaging.

3. My actions before:

Resentful of the workload expected. I spoke negatively about him to others in the office.

4. My attitude after:
I became bitter toward him. I still have resentment toward him.

5. My reactions after:
I slandered him to other workers and to my family. I gossiped. I became slothful in the way I did my work. I purposely did . . . to sabotage him.

6. The effects of my choices on my life and relationships since then:
I live in fear at my current job that my boss is going to do the same thing to me. It causes me to dread going to work, and I find myself avoiding any contact with my boss that is not absolutely necessary. I hate going to work.

7. What I should have done:
I should have spoken to him honestly and respectfully about how he treats me. I should have sought his input into anything I am not doing in my work that he expects of me. I should have continued to do my work to the best of my ability as long as I was employed there. I should not have retaliated with gossip and slander and seeking to sabotage him, but to pray for him and seek to help him.

Example of Completed Marriage Inventory Worksheet:

1. What happened in my marriage?
My wife had an affair with my best friend in 1998.

2. My attitude before:
I took for granted that she would always love me and be there for me. I thought of her as my personal servant and housekeeper.

3. My actions before:
I spent way too much time pursuing my own interests. I worked more than I should have, and when I wasn't working, I did recreational things I wanted to do. I always put her low on the list of my priorities.

4. My attitude after:
I hated her for betraying me and humiliating me. I felt no woman could ever be trusted and that I would never trust another woman again.

5. My reactions after:
I had an affair of my own just to show her. I have held women off at arm's length so they can't hurt me. I treat women as objects.

6. The effects of my choices on my life and relationships since then:

I have been unable to feel at ease with any woman whom I have dated since. They always tell me they can't seem to get to know me. Eventually they lose interest and turn to someone else.

7. What I should have done:

I should have been more attentive to my wife during our marriage. I should have known that to go out and do the same thing she had done was not going to hurt her, but hurt me and dishonor God. I should have forgiven her (released her from my debt) so I could go on with my life without this mistrust, bitterness, and anger.

As you can see by the examples, these inventory worksheets provide an opportunity for you to be brutally honest with yourself. A blank Marriage Inventory Worksheet and General Life Inventory Worksheet are provided at the end of this chapter.

What is the most important thing you have learned in this step?

____

____

____

____

What are you going to do in your marriage this week as a result of this step?

____

____

____

____

____

____

____

TABLE TALK

What is the most important thing about you, that relates to this chapter, that you are going to share with your spouse this week?

____

____

____

____

MARRIAGE INVENTORY WORKSHEET

1. Circumstance: What happened in my marriage?

____

____

____

____

2. **My attitude before:** ______________________________

3. My actions before: ______________________________

4. My attitudes after: ______________________________

5. My reactions after: ______________________________

6. The effects of my choices on my life and relationships since then:

____

____

____

____

7. What I should have done: ______________________________

Using this form, continue on your own paper. Be aware that you will not be able to complete this inventory in one week. Continue doing the inventory as you and the group move on to the other steps. This inventory may take some time to complete.

GENERAL LIFE INVENTORY WORKSHEET

1. Circumstance: What happened and who was involved?

____

____

____

____

2. My attitude before: ______________________________

3. My actions before: ______________________________

4. My attitudes after: ______________________________

5. My reactions after: ______________________________

6. The effects of my choices on my life and relationships since then:

____

____

____

____

7. What I should have done: __________________________

Using this form, continue on your own paper. Be aware that you will not be able to complete this inventory in one week. Continue doing the inventory as you and the group move on to the other steps. This inventory may take months to complete.

JOURNAL

9

"E"—Expose the Secrets

"Admitted to God, to ourselves, and to another human being, the exact nature of our wrongs."

THE PROBLEM OF "E"

I grew up in the outdoors. Fishing has always been one of my favorite outdoor things to do. Through the years, I have owned several different boats. Since bass fishing is the kind of fishing I love the most, on every boat I have always had a trolling motor on the front end. A trolling motor allows you to move quietly, because it is electrically powered, and it also allows you to get into shallow water where the big motor can't be operated. A few years ago, I began to notice that my trolling motor just wasn't pulling my boat like it once had. I thought maybe I needed a new battery, so I got a new one. That didn't help. I thought perhaps the motor was going bad. But it wasn't really old enough for that to be the problem. I became so frustrated that I was just about to scrap the thing and get a new one when I decided to take the propeller off and see if I could find something there that might be causing the problem. When I pulled off the propeller, I knew immediately what my problem had been all along. Fishing line was wrapped around the shaft of the propeller and was preventing it from turning freely! When I removed the fishing line, it ran like a brand new motor! Until I brought the propeller up out of the water so it could be seen, nothing I did made any difference. It had to be exposed in order to be solved.

The point is, what is hidden hurts. What is hidden has the power to drag us down and prevent us from moving forward, just like that fishing line around the propeller. It has to be exposed in order to be removed. In step four, we discovered the problem. The problem was the barnacles beneath the water line or the string around the propeller. In this step, we start the process of removing the line, and that begins with bringing it to the surface so it can be exposed. The challenge of this step is simply our fear of exposure. We are afraid for others to know our hidden secrets because of what they might think of us. We fear people knowing the truth about what is really wrapped around our propeller. This is nothing but image management. While we are doing image management, we are living a lie. We are living in darkness with hidden secrets, and until those secrets are exposed, they will continue to create fear and have power over our lives.

That is what secrets do, isn't it? Secrets keep us in their power because we live in constant fear that someone is going to discover the secret. I can strip the secret of its power when I no longer have fear it might be discovered. If I have already exposed it, no one can discover it. They say to me, "I found out something about you." When they tell me what it is, I can reply, "Is that all you've got? That's old news. I brought that out into the open a long time ago. If you intend to use something to hurt me, it is going to have to be better than that one." I don't have to live in fear of being found out if I have already taken the initiative to expose it to God, others, and myself.

This truth can be expressed in several ways. "We are only as sick as our secrets." This is true. "Secrets make us sick and we are as sick as the secrets we keep." Another way of saying it is, "Secrets put bullets in the enemy's gun to shoot us with!" As long as I keep secrets, I am arming the very one who is out to destroy me. I help my Enemy by keeping secrets. The way to disarm the Enemy, who wants to shoot me, is take all of his ammunition away. Empty his gun so that when he pulls the trigger, nothing happens. This step in the process is the first step of exposure. It isn't the end, but the beginning. There will be further steps of exposure later on. But here, I take the first step when I confess the secrets to myself, God, and one other human being.

Our text for Step 5 is found in Step 4. In that step, we discovered some attitudes and actions that were destructive and harmful to others and ourselves. We took a searching and fearless moral inventory and wrote it down. This is what we confess in Step 5. If you didn't make a sincere effort at moral inventory, then there is no need to continue. Perhaps you should go back and take another stab at the discovery step.

If you have made that effort, even though there may be things you didn't remember, you are ready to begin the exposing process. More attitudes and actions will come to you as you move into this part of the process.

What is one thing you discovered in Step 4 that you are the most reluctant to confess?

____

____

____

What is it that you fear about confessing that one thing?

____

____

____

____

What would it feel like if you were at a place where you had no fear of others knowing that about you?

____

____

____

____

THE PROCESS OF "E"

What Is Confession?

Getting Honest

As mentioned in chapter one, the Greek word for "confess" means literally to "speak the same as." It has the idea of "coming into agreement." When the Bible speaks about "confessing" to God, it doesn't mean telling Him something He doesn't already know! It means we are finally coming into agreement with Him about what He already knows. The same is true with ourselves. Deep inside, we all know that many of our attitudes and actions are wrong, destructive, and need to be changed. But there is always another side of us that wants to rationalize, justify, and even deny that truth. When we confess to ourselves, we are coming into open agreement with what we already know deep down inside. We are getting honest. When this happens, we begin to be released from the inner conflict that has resulted in so much tension.

When we confess to others, we discover that what we thought was a huge secret wasn't really all that secret after all. We discover that other people already know a great deal about what we thought we had kept secret. If I am a controlling person, others already know it. If I harbor anger and resentment in my heart, it doesn't take other people around me long to figure it out. If I am insecure, or have a low sense of self-worth, people (for the most part) figure it out pretty soon. They may never tell me about it or indicate they are aware of it, but they usually are. I begin to discover that what I thought were hidden things were in fact "open secrets" all along. Bringing it all out in the open in confession allows me to live openly, with honesty and integrity, and in that environment, real change can happen.

Confession, at its core, involves at least three things. When these three are recognized and embraced fully, then our confession becomes full, honest, and genuine.

Ownership of Responsibility

When we confess, we are by definition accepting responsibility for our thoughts, attitudes, and actions. Though there may have been traumatic experiences in the past for which we were not responsible that have wounded us and set us up for some of the attitudes that now plague us, confession means that we now take full ownership and responsibility for the choices we have made. If we are ever to get beyond the wounds of the past, we must accept responsibility for our own choices. The pathway to maturity is from irresponsibility to responsibility.

In 2009, the head basketball coach of Louisville University, Rick Patino, admitted that he had an inappropriate sexual relationship with a woman other than his wife. It had already turned into a huge mess for everyone involved. Lies had been told, a cover-up had begun, and everything had gone from bad to worse. Patino eventually came clean and admitted the affair. In a press conference he made a statement that sums up ownership of responsibility and the importance of confessing the truth. He said, "When you have a problem, if you tell the truth, the problem becomes a part of your past. If you lie it becomes a part of your future."[1] This part of the process is the beginning of putting destructive things in your rear-view mirror! Putting them in your past keeps them from being a part of your present and future.

Entering the Pain

Part of accepting responsibility means that we are willing to enter the pain our attitudes and actions have caused others. Often, we leave in our wake a battlefield strewn with the bodies of those who have become casualties of our attitudes and actions. In confession, we are faced with the reality that our choices have caused pain, not only to ourselves, but also to God and others. It is a fact that our sinful attitudes and choices never affect only us. They bring pain to the heart of God and usually into the lives of others. As you have reviewed your life experience, perhaps you have realized it was the sinful actions of others that wounded you, either in childhood or adulthood.

1. Rick Patino, ESPN News Conference, August 12, 2009.

You were affected by their sinful choices. In the same way, your sinful choices have caused pain to others. Confession means that you are willing to enter into that pain and acknowledge it.

Taking a Risk on Grace

Confession is a risk. What if the other person isn't willing to forgive? What if they use my honesty against me? Anytime you confess, you are taking a risk on grace. Is it possible that you could take this risk and be hurt? With human beings, it is always possible, but with God it is not. He has promised to give grace when we humbly come before Him.

> *God is opposed to the proud but gives grace to the humble. (James 4:6)*

At the end of this step, we will give some guidelines about how to decide which person you will confess to. Not everyone is qualified to hear you and extend grace. You must use wisdom in deciding with whom you will share your confession. It must be someone who is capable of, and willing to express, grace.

Now it is time to begin taking this step in the adventure. We will begin by discussing what confession in each of these directions means, what results are possible, and how to go about completing this step of the process.

Confession in 3-D

Have you ever seen a movie in 3-D? You go into the theater, and they give you those funny plastic glasses to wear. You put them on and feel a little dumb at first. But, when the movie begins, all that goes away because suddenly you realize this is completely different from one-dimensional viewing. Things come off the screen right at you! Everything seems more alive and realistic. In fact, 3-D viewing makes you feel that you are a part of the action.

Confession in its fullness is also a 3-D experience. You can do one-dimensional and even two-dimensional confession, but you don't get the full experience until you experience confession in 3-D. By three-dimensional, we mean that full confession has to go in three directions. To self, others, and to God. Honesty and integrity are vital to healthy relationships in all three directions. Inward to ourselves. Outward toward others. Upward toward the heavenly Father.

> **Principle: Relationships thrive in the light of honesty. Relationships die in the darkness of deception.**

In 1 John 1, the apostle develops the principle of honesty in these three directions. First, he sets the stage with a statement about God in verse 5.

This is the message we have heard from Him and announce to you, that God is Light, and in Him there is no darkness at all. (1 John 1:5)

In other words, God, at His core, is light. What does this mean? When you contrast that to the Enemy, Satan, you can begin to get an idea. Jesus said of the Enemy that he is a "liar and the father of lies" (John 8:44). In other words, at his core he is deception. A liar, filled with the opposite of light, which is darkness.

John spoke of Jesus who came into the world as the Light of the world and what the world did with the Light and why they did it.

This is the judgment, that the Light has come into the world, and men loved the darkness rather than the Light, for their deeds were evil. (John 3:19)

The picture is beginning to take shape. Men whose deeds are evil did not want them brought into the Light so they hated the Light. They wanted their deeds hidden, covered up, so they sought to destroy the Light.

Light by its nature dispels darkness. It reveals what is in the darkness. If you walk into a dark room and flip on the light switch everything in the room is revealed. The opposite is also true. If you switch the light off, everything in the room becomes hidden. Men, the Scripture says, hated the Light because their deeds were evil and did not want them revealed. Jesus switched on the Light and men hated it.

First John 1:5 tells us that, in God's character, there is no deception, no darkness, only the light of honesty and truth. In the Enemy's character there is no truth, no light, only the darkness of deception.

God does His work in our lives as we walk in the Light, not the darkness. Walking in the Light doesn't mean being perfect. Walking in the Light means walking in honesty and integrity with ourselves, each other, and with God. Honesty in 3-D. In the next five verses John develops the need for honesty, integrity, and confession in three directions.

Getting Honest with Ourselves

If we say that we have fellowship with Him and yet walk in the darkness, we lie and do not practice the truth . . . If we say that we have no sin, we are deceiving ourselves, and the truth is not in us. (1 John 1:6, 8)

We have to get honest with ourselves first. Dishonesty with self is called denial. All integrity and honesty begins at home. Within myself. I have to quit deceiving myself.

You have already gotten started in the right direction because in the last leg you did a searching and fearless moral inventory. You went back and inventoried your entire life in the area of attitudes and actions using the Seven Deadly Sins and Fruit of the Spirit as a guide. You were completely honest with yourself . . . or were you? Were there some things that at the time you could not bring yourself to admit, even to yourself? Take a moment right now to think about that. Is there anything you left out?

Review your moral inventory and write down anything you can think of that you didn't recall in the fourth leg of the adventure.

____

____

____

____

A necessary part of healing from trauma or loss is to move through a grief process. You have to allow yourself to experience the pain and grief in order to ever move beyond it. In other words, grief is part of the healing process. Admitting to yourself the true nature of your wrongs is to allow yourself the freedom to enter into the grief process. It means to experience the pain and remorse, and allow yourself to grieve over the thought or action and the negative consequences it has brought into your life or the lives of others. As you review your moral inventory, pick out several things on the list that you feel the most regret about. Allow yourself to be released for a few moments to experience your grief over that. Cry if you need to. Scream if it helps. Maybe just sit quietly and allow yourself to contemplate how you feel.

In the best way you can, use words or a picture image to express how you are feeling right now.

____

____

____

____

Getting Honest with God

If we say that we have no sin, we are deceiving ourselves and the truth is not in us. If we confess our sins, He is faithful and righteous to forgive us our sins and to cleanse us of all unrighteousness. (1 John 1:8–9)

The truth this verse reveals is that we are all guilty. Romans 3:23 agrees with this assessment when it says, "for all have sinned and fall short of the glory of God!" The result is real guilt before God. The problem with guilt is that it can be incredibly destructive if it isn't resolved. There are two kinds of guilt. First, there is real guilt before God because of sin. This is the guilt about which the Bible speaks. We are all guilty before Him. Second is imposed guilt that we put on ourselves. This guilt is irrational and unjustified. Sometimes, because of experiences in life, we can become a guilt magnet. We develop the habit of taking on guilt for everything that happens around us, regardless of whether we have any real culpability or not. God wants us to be set free from both kinds of guilt. Why? Because unresolved guilt, whether it is real or self-imposed, is destructive.

It has even been said that the most destructive force in the human experience is unresolved guilt. Some counselors and psychiatrists have even surmised that if people could just resolve their guilt issues, psychiatric hospitals and counselors would go out of business. This may be an overstatement, but it does reflect the incredible toll that unresolved guilt has taken (and is taking) on human beings.

In the Old Testament, King David acknowledged the toll of unresolved guilt in his life when he refused to acknowledge and confess his own sin.

Be gracious to me, O Lord, for I am in distress; my eye is wasted away from grief, my soul and my body also. For my life is spent with sorrow and my years with sighing; my strength has failed because of my iniquity, and my body has wasted away. (Psalms 31:9–10)

However, just one psalm later, David acknowledged the release that confession had accomplished in his life.

I acknowledged my sin to You, and my iniquity I did not hide; I said, "I will confess my transgressions to the Lord"; and You forgave the guilt of my sin. (Psalms 32:5)

In this fifth leg of the journey, it is time to take your moral inventory before God and confess it. As you do, allow yourself to experience His cleansing and forgiveness, and be set free from your guilt. He intends to set you free from both the guilt that He has declared is real because of your sin, and the guilt you have taken on unnecessarily.

Let us draw near with a sincere heart in full assurance of faith, having our hearts sprinkled clean from an evil conscience . . . (Hebrews 10:22)

Guilt is such a destructive force in our lives. God knows that guilt prevents us from experiencing the joy and freedom He desires for us. This is why He offers to us so willingly His forgiveness and freedom from guilt.

One of the most destructive results of guilt in our lives is the fear it creates. When we are holding on to guilt, we live in fear that we will be found out. This fear becomes a prison that keeps us from living life with confidence. In fact, the fear that comes from guilt affects every area of our lives. It has its most devastating effects on our ability to relate to others with integrity, honesty, and intimacy. When we are afraid that others will find us out, we cannot be open and free with them. We spend valuable time and emotional energy keeping up the façade.

A parable is told of a Jewish couple living under the Nazi regime who were anticipating their eventual arrest. They made plans for the care of their son. An agreement was made with a man who would care for the boy when they were arrested. In return, he was to receive as payment the paid-up lease on the couple's apartment. As expected, they eventually were arrested. The man promptly smuggled the boy away to a remote location and left him there to fend for himself. He then sold the lease on the apartment and kept the money for himself. Then one morning, he noticed a lump about the size of a pigeon's egg that had arisen on his forehead. He pressed the bump, and it disappeared only to pop up again on the back of his head. He pushed it again and it showed up over his ear. He finally pressed it and it popped up on the top of his head. He felt that this was a distinct improvement because he could at least cover it with his hat! However, the rest of his life he lived with the disconcerting anticipation that it would someday move again and someone would come up to him and say, "Your lump is showing!"

The parable illustrates the debilitating effect of guilt. We try to cover it up, hide it, or stuff it down inside. Then we live our lives with the fear that it's going to someday show itself and others are going to find out. When we refuse to confess our sin to God we are calling God a liar.

If we say that we have not sinned, we make Him a liar, and His word is not in us. (1 John 1:10)

The meaning of that verse follows from 1 John 1:9: "If we confess our sins, He is faithful and righteous to forgive us." Once again, "confess" in the original language means to "speak the same as." In other words, God has seen my wrong attitudes and actions and has already called them what they are—sins. He is just waiting for me to "speak the same as" He has spoken about it and agree with Him. That's confession before God. I don't inform Him of something He doesn't already know. I agree with Him in what He has already declared to be true. Then, I am walking in the Light before God—the light of honesty with Him.

What is the one thing you feel guilty about that you have always feared someone else would find out? (You listed this on the second page of this step.)

____

____

____

____

Confession is the first step toward being set free from the fear that guilt creates. Tell it to God. Remember, He already knows. He is just waiting for you to come into agreement with Him about the nature of your wrongs. Allow Him now to give you release, forgiveness, and freedom.

Using your inventory, take these things to God one by one and acknowledge them before Him. Ask for and receive His forgiveness once and for all. Remember, you must take Him at His word that when you genuinely confess to Him and are broken over your sin, He forgives!

> *If we confess our sins, He is faithful and righteous to forgive us our sins and to cleanse us from all unrighteousness. (1 John 1:9)*

Now that you have gotten honest with God, write something about your experience of understanding and receiving God's unconditional love and mercy in your life.

____

____

____

____

____

Getting Honest with Others

I want to make two applications of this third dimension of confession. The first application is related to the text in 1 John.

Living in Integrity with Others

But if we walk in the Light as He Himself is in the Light, we have fellowship with one another, and the blood of Jesus His Son cleanses us from all sin. (1 John 1:7)

John uses the word "fellowship" in this verse. This is the word the New Testament uses to describe the community that believers have together in Christ. It means literally "sharing in common." It refers to doing life and ministry together in Christ. What allows us to have fellowship is that we are both walking in the Light. Once again, walking in the Light doesn't mean perfection. It means honesty, truth, and integrity. When one of us walks in the darkness of deception with the other, fellowship becomes impossible. Darkness and light cannot exist together. The relationship is bound to deteriorate.

However, when we walk in the Light, notice what John says the blood of Jesus does. It cleanses us from all sin! We know about the cleansing power of Jesus' blood in our relationship to God. Our salvation depends upon it. However, our relationship to one another also depends upon it. That's the context in which John makes this reference. When we walk in the Light—in other words, when we are honest with one another and relate to one another with truth and integrity—we can apply the cleansing blood of Christ to our relationship as we forgive one another in our failings, hurt feelings, misunderstandings, etc. But once one of us injects deception into the relationship by lying, withholding the truth of what we feel, or think happened in the relationship, we negate the cleansing power of the blood of Christ in the relationship. Then darkness and death are introduced into the relationship, and it is sure to fail.

This is true of any relationship. It is true of members of the body of Christ with one another. It is true of friendships. It is certainly true in marriage. When lack of honesty and integrity is introduced into the marriage relationship, it begins to die.

Living in Transparency with Others

Therefore confess your sins to one another, and pray for one another, so that you may be healed. (James 5:16)

It would be easy to say, "Well, I have confessed this to myself and to God, and nobody else ever needs to know about it." The danger this presents is that it continues to feed our desire to conceal. Remember, "We are only as sick as our secrets." Things that live in the shadows and the darkness are things that we fear. Anything that we fear has some control over us. To be released from fear and control, we have to bring the secrets out into full light. In the light, they lose their power. There is healing power in sharing honestly with another person, and experiencing grace and acceptance from them. In fact, we often find that our secrets are not that much different from others' secrets. We are all fallen creatures and in need of grace.

Perhaps you have noticed that the first four steps have focused on you and God. You admitted powerless in Step 1. In Step 2, you began to examine what you believed about God, yourself, and others. In Step 3, you committed your will and life to Christ, and in Step 4 you discovered destructive attitudes and actions in your moral inventory.

So far, it has just been you and God. However, beginning with Step 5, you must include others. It begins with only one other person at this point. Later, in Step 9, you include all the people with whom you need to make direct amends. In Step 12, you include every person who is willing to hear your story of *help*, *hope*, and *healing*. In fact, this pattern is reflected in Jesus' commissioning of the disciples just before He ascended to the heavens.

> *"But you will receive power when the Holy Spirit has come upon you; and you shall be My witnesses both in Jerusalem, and in all Judea and Samaria, and even to the remotest part of the earth." (Acts 1:8)*

It was to begin at home and expand from there until it eventually encompassed the whole earth. That pattern is reflected in this process of including others in our growth. It begins with one, but eventually needs to expand to anyone who will become a part of the process. In fact, in this truth is found the reason why it isn't enough to just confess to ourselves and to God. We must become connected in community with others in order to experience God's true *help*, *hope*, and *healing*.

The Christian life cannot be lived in isolation from others. Living as a Christian is a team sport by God's design! In fact, there are more than twenty "one another" commands we can't obey unless we are connected in community with other believers. Love one another, pray for one another, encourage one another, and bear one another's burdens.

When we come to James 5:16, we are told to "confess . . . [our] sins to one another." The idea that I can grow as a Christian, mature as a Christian, and become what God wants me to be by limiting the process to just God and me is a denial of what Scripture says.

I don't pretend to have full understanding of why God has decreed this to be true, but I am convinced it is what the Scripture says. However, I do understand a practical reason why it is true in the area of healing our hurts and wounds in life.

The vast majority of our hurts in life have come from people. It is people who have wounded us, and then we have wounded other people. Those wounds have created all kinds of negative attitudes and actions on our part. Things such as resentment, anger, mistrust, and unforgiveness. If wounds come from people, it makes a great deal of practical sense that God would use people to bring the healing and growth.

For example, if someone has been thrown from a horse and has developed a fear of horses, the only way to overcome that fear is to get back up on a horse. A horse brought about the hurt, and a horse has to be a part of the healing. If a person has been burned and has developed a fear of fire, the only way to overcome that fear is to be in contact with fire.

So, people have hurt us, and God intends to use people to heal us. He works through people. Therefore, if we refuse to reach out and include people in the process of growth and healing, then we are refusing God's help. You might be thinking, "But if I open myself up to people again, someone might hurt me again." There is no "might" about it. Others will hurt you again, and you will hurt others again, either intentionally or unintentionally. It is only a question of when. Life in this fallen world is a process of hurting and healing, hurting and healing, hurting and healing. It will always be so until we are in heaven with Christ. The real question is, "Will you only be hurt or will you allow God to bring healing?" If you will, you must allow others to be a part of the process.

For years, I have contemplated the design of the dreaded hospital gown. Who came up with this thing? Is it some hangover from medieval times? Is it someone's idea of a sick joke? Could it be that this gown is the spawn of Satan himself? Probably not, but I never met anyone who liked the thing. It wasn't designed for making a fashion statement, that's for sure. Neither was it designed with the modest person in mind. The designer of the hospital gown had one goal. Easy access. The gown is designed to make getting to the nether regions of the body as easy for the caregivers as humanly possible, just short of the patient being in his or her birthday suit.

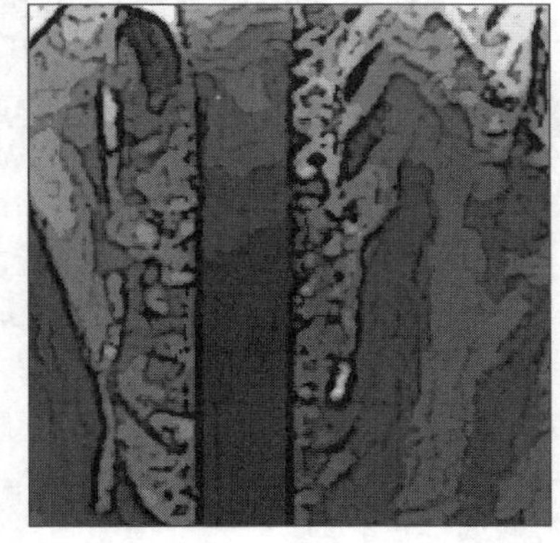

It's interesting how for the first few days in the hospital, the patient tries to hold onto at least a little bit of his/her dignity. He keeps the gown pulled down over his knees and is careful to keep the flaps in the back overlapping. After a few days in the hospital, after being poked and prodded over every part of his body, the caution seems to fade away. You see a guy walking down the hall with the back wide open and flapping in the breeze, and he couldn't care less. He figures by this time, everyone in the place has already seen everything. Why hide anything? He feels safe and free.

A few years ago, one of our elders nearly died on an overseas business trip. He had massive internal hemorrhaging and needed surgery, but he didn't want to have it overseas. They worked for several days to get him stable enough to fly back to the States. He eventually had surgery to remove a good portion of his stomach, which was ulcerated. It was a grueling three-week stay in the hospital. He has a loving wife and grown children, so he was constantly in their care. Almost every time I went by the hospital, someone was there with him. We would sit and talk. I would feed him ice chips because he couldn't drink water for a while after his surgery. Sometimes, he would be in intense pain and we would pray. Once, when I left his room, I knew he was in great pain, but he was doing his best to keep a positive attitude and not complain. I leaned over and kissed him on his bearded cheek. I don't make a practice of kissing other men, but I felt moved with compassion for him. I figured he wouldn't remember it anyway. I was wrong. He did remember. We have laughed about it since.

One day near the end of his stay, I was sitting beside his bed. There happened to be no one else in the room at the time. He was far enough along in his recovery that he was able to get out of bed some and walk around. He said, "I need to go to the bathroom." So he rolled out of the bed, on the opposite side from me, and stood facing away from me. I'm telling you, when he stood up wearing that hospital gown with his back to me . . . well, how do I say this delicately? There was a full moon right there in front of me! Not a half moon. Not a quarter moon. A full moon in all of its glory right there. I started laughing, and I laughed 'til I almost cried. He couldn't have cared less. He had been poked and prodded for three weeks. He felt totally uninhibited and safe to bare it all. That is the true essence of "exposing oneself."

Since that experience, I have told the story many times, and each time I tell it, I am moved with the thought, "Wouldn't it be wonderful if our lives were such an open book that we could live with that kind of uninhibited abandon?" No secrets, no fear. That is the goal. Step 5 is a small, first step in the right direction.

What is your greatest hesitation about sharing your inventory with another person?

____

____

____

____

____

____

____

Who Do You Tell?

Choosing whom you are going to tell is as important as becoming willing to tell someone in the first place. So whom should you tell?

1. Someone you can trust.

This person needs to be someone who can keep a confidence. What you are going to tell does not need to be repeated unless you choose to repeat it.

2. Someone who can understand.

Someone who has already walked through this process will always be able to understand what you are doing. This may mean that you need to select someone who has already gone through a freedom group process or is currently doing so.

3. Someone mature enough to handle your confession.

Someone significantly younger than you may not be a good choice. Even someone your own age who is emotionally immature would not be a good choice. You need to choose someone who is mature enough to take seriously the trust you are placing in him or her.

4. Someone who can reflect God's grace to you.

Once again, this points toward someone who has been through the process. Someone who has experienced grace is usually someone who can extend it. Also, this person should be someone who would not be personally hurt or damaged by what you tell them. That would make it difficult for them to express acceptance and grace. A spouse or family member is not a recommended person for this process. The best person is someone who does not have a strong emotional investment in you. That person can listen objectively, without condemnation, judgment, or hurt.

5. Someone of the same gender.

It is usually more appropriate and comfortable to talk to someone of the same gender.

Now it's time to finish this leg of the journey. Who are you going to tell? Using the suggestions above, write the names of two or three people whom you feel would be appropriate to tell. Write them in order of your personal preference.

____

____

____

Now select one person you will ask to hear your step "D" inventory.

____

What do you feel you can reasonably expect from this person?

____

____

____

____

What do you have to lose? If you stop here and do not finish this leg of the journey, what are you going to miss? How about the experience of forgiveness, freedom from your guilt, and grace? What do you have to lose if you go through the process? How about your sense of isolation as you discover that you are not alone in the problems you face? You have your sense of denial to lose. Confessing honestly brings everything out in the open so you can deal with the real issues. Your implanted pride. When you see yourself as you really are and see God as He really is, then pride has no place to stand in your life. Your unwillingness to forgive others. When you are accepted and forgiven for your wrongs, you will suddenly find that you are more able and willing to forgive others. Those are the things you have to lose. Let them go! Say *adios*! Good riddance!

Now Set a Time and Go Do It!

After completing this leg of the journey, pray to God to disclose to you anything you may have left out. If you remember something, make another appointment with the person with whom you did this step to expose what you previously had excluded.

After you have done Step 5, write out how you feel. What was the experience like?

____

____

____

____

____

What is the most important thing you have learned in this chapter?

____

____

____

____

What do you plan to do in your marriage this week as a result of this step?

____

____

____

____

TABLE TALK

What is the most important thing about you that relates to this chapter, that you are going to share with your spouse this week?

JOURNAL

10

"F"—Focus on Faith

"We were entirely ready to have God remove all these defects of character. Humbly asked Him to remove our shortcomings."

THE PROBLEM OF "F"

Recently, I went to Costa Rica to check out a mission opportunity for our church. While I was there, the guy who was showing me the mission said that I couldn't leave Costa Rica without doing the longest zip line in the world. My wife has accused me of being an adrenalin junkie, and so my response was immediately, "I'm in!" They take you up a mountain on a lift and then, for the next two hours, you zip down eight separate legs of the line. The first two legs are fairly short, so you can get the system down, and then they begin to stretch out. In fact, several of the legs are a half-mile long! You are flying over the top of the rain forest at 50 miles per hour hanging onto a bar attached to a cable (with safety straps). As you prepare to leave the platform for each leg of the journey, the guide checks all your hook-ups and then asks, "*listo*?" And you reply, "*listo*." Then it's "*adios muchacho*!" and away you go. The word *listo* is Spanish for "ready." He's asking, "Are you ready?"

That is the question that is asked in this step of the process. *Listo*? Are you ready? Are you ready to have your defects removed? This is an important question, isn't it? I suspect that if you have really done the first five steps with diligence and honesty, you are more than ready to have your defects removed.

What character defects do you most want removed?

1. ______________________________

2. ______________________________

3. ______________________________

What pain have they caused you and others in your life?

____

Totalmente Listo? (Entirely Ready?)

Notice this step says we are "entirely ready." Not just ready, but entirely ready. Full readiness is vital. If you haven't honestly and seriously done the first five steps, perhaps you are not entirely ready. If you can't sincerely say you are ready to have God make these changes, I suggest you go back through the first five steps and look at the choices, the consequences, and the pain these things have caused you and others. This time, look at them and allow yourself to feel the pain for real. The truth is, sometimes we fear change, even when we really hate where we are, simply because at least the misery we are in is familiar. It's familiar misery, and we know what to expect from it. We don't know what life would be like without it, and that is what causes us to be uncertain. We have to get over that hesitation. We have to come to the place where we detest the defect, and the pain it has caused in our lives and the lives of loved ones around us, so much that we are willing to face the uncertainty of change.

Before you can ask God to remove these shortcomings, you have to want them to be removed. Your wants have to have changed. If your wants haven't been changed yet, then before you can ask Him to change your character, why not ask God to change your wants? Say to Him, "I'm not really sure I want them removed, but I want to want them removed." Until your wants are truly changed, the asking will be ineffective. So, if that is where you honestly are, and you pray honestly about your wants, I believe He will respond to that simple and honest request. He wants to change your wants.

Are there any character defects you are not sure you want God to remove?

____

____

____

____

What fears do you have about having these things removed?

____

____

____

____

____

What can you imagine your life (marriage) would be like without these character defects?

____

____

____

____

What difference would it make for the people closest to you if God removed your defects?

____

____

____

____

THE PROCESS OF "F"

Beyond our fear of failure, this step poses another great challenge—understanding what faith really is. This is a faith step. In this step we are asking God to do something. We are asking Him to remove our character defects. In fact, it is the only step in the process where we are directly asking Him to do something. In the other steps, we are committing ourselves to do what He has told us to do. Now we are about to ask Him to do something for us. That makes this a faith step.

In order for us to do this step, we must have some understanding of what faith is! What does it mean to have faith? What does it mean to ask in faith? Scripture says over and over that when we ask God, we must "ask in faith" in order to receive.

But he must ask in faith without any doubting . . . (James 1:6)

In the eleventh chapter of Hebrews, the great faith chapter, it states in verse 6, "Without faith it is impossible to please Him." Certainly we want to please Him, and in this step we are asking Him for something that we desperately need and desire. Since we must "ask in faith" to receive what we are asking, we certainly better understand what faith is! Without turning this into a theology lesson, I need to spend some time answering that question because there is much confusion and misunderstanding about the nature of true faith.

The Essence of Faith

Faith Is a Channel

Faith is the channel by which we receive what God desires to give. Notice I said, "What God desires to give." In other words, faith is not a tool we use to change God's mind. It isn't a magic wand that we can wave and get anything from God we want for ourselves regardless of whether it is something He desires to give or not. Faith is the channel through which we receive what He desires to give us.

For by grace you have been saved through faith . . . (Ephesians 2:8)

Notice that grace is what we receive. Grace is the free gift of salvation through Jesus Christ. We don't deserve salvation. We can't earn salvation. It's a gift of God. Grace. That's what God desires to give us—grace. The passage says that we receive this gift of grace "through faith." Faith is the channel through which we receive what God desires to give. If that is true, then it is very important that we clearly understand what this channel of faith really is. Faith entails several things.

Faith Is an Action Not a Thought

True biblical faith is not nearly as mysterious as many want to make it. In fact, faith is very practical. Faith is not positive thinking. Faith is not a thought at all. Faith is action! Faith is not something you think or feel, faith is something you do. Faith always requires that I do something. In fact, I would go as far as to say that, "Faith is an action, and faith results in action."

What use is it, my brethren, if someone says he has faith but he has no works? Can that faith save Him? . . . But are you willing to recognize, you foolish fellow, that faith without works is useless? (James 2:14, 20)

This text claims that faith that doesn't result in action isn't real faith. In fact, this verse says that kind of faith is useless. It won't accomplish anything. The works that follow faith are not what saves. Only faith saves, and the works that follow faith prove the quality and reality of genuine faith.

An illustration of this aspect of faith is like the story that we began chapter 7 (Step "C", Commit to Christ) with, but with a little different twist. It's the story of an acrobat who stretched a cable across Niagara Falls and pushed a wheelbarrow back and forth across that cable with the raging falls beneath. On one end a man was watching him perform this incredible feat of courage and balance. The acrobat asked the man, "Do you believe I can push this wheelbarrow across the falls without falling off?" The man replied, "Of course, I believe you can." To which the acrobat replied, "Then get in the wheelbarrow." At that moment, the man's "faith" was put to the acid test. Was it just words, or would it result in the action of getting in the wheelbarrow? In that situation, faith wouldn't be thinking the man could do it. It wouldn't be saying the man could do it. Faith would be getting into the wheelbarrow and letting the man push you across the falls.

In fact, as you read Hebrews 11, you will repeatedly hear the phrase, "by faith . . .," and then it tells what the individual did by faith. "By faith Abraham . . ., by faith Noah . . ." And then it tells what Noah did by faith. The list goes on and on throughout the chapter. For each person, faith resulted in action. That aspect of faith is clear.

The other aspect of faith, however, is not as clear. What action is faith? The action that is faith is the action of taking God at His word. Return to Ephesians 2:8: "For by grace you have been saved through faith." God has said He sent His Son, Jesus Christ, to be a perfect sacrifice for sins. He has promised to forgive sins for all who come to Him through His Son, Jesus Christ. John 1:12 says, "As many as received Him, to them He gave the right to become children of God." So, as an individual, I must hear what God has said about the way of forgiveness and salvation, and I must "take Him at His word" and receive Christ as my savior. I simply do what He said I should do! That's faith.

Once again, I refer you to the faith chapter in Hebrews where Abraham is mentioned (vv. 11:8–10). In the Old Testament book of Genesis, God spoke to Abraham and said if Abraham would leave Ur, the land of the Chaldees, and go where God would lead him, God would give him that land and would multiply his descendants and through him create a great nation through which He would bless all of the nations of the earth. That was the birth of the Hebrew nation—when Abraham did what God told him to do. He believed what God had said. He took God at His word that God would do what He promised He would do. So, Abraham packed up and went to the land that God showed him.

Principle: You cannot have faith apart from the Word of God. God must speak first before you can take Him at His word.

So faith comes from hearing, and hearing by the word of Christ. (Romans 10:17)

Abraham took God at His word when God's word came to him. He was faced with a choice. Will I take God at His word that He will do what He has promised He will do? If I take Him at His word, then I have to do what He has told me to do. If I don't take Him at His word and don't do what He has told me to do, then I will stay right where I am in Ur of the Chaldees.

The acrobat at the falls tells me he can push me across the falls without plunging me to my death below. Do I take him at his word or not? Whether I get into the wheelbarrow or not depends upon whether I take him at his word or not. In other words, "Faith isn't saying you believe something God has said in His Word. Faith is acting upon (obeying) what He has said in His Word."

What Is Faith?

Faith is an ______________________________ through

which we receive what God ______________________________

to ______________________________ us. Faith is taking

God ______________________________.

The Premise and the Promise

The Bible is filled with the promises of God. There is so much God wants to give us when we become His children through faith in Jesus Christ, and these are His promises to us. Just as any good earthly parents desire to give their children good things—things that are good for them—so also our heavenly Father desires to give His children good things. These are His promises that He gives to us in His Word. But notice, God's promises always come with a premise. The promise is what He wants to do. The premise is what He wants me to do in order to receive the promise. It's at the intersection of the promise and the premise that faith either happens or doesn't. Sometimes it helps to have a visual illustration of truth.

He promises if I will do what He wants me to do, then He will do something good for me that He wants to do. In essence, He wants me, as His child, to put my life into a place where He, as my Father, can legitimately bless me with good things. At the intersection of the premise and the promise, I will choose to obey Him (faith) and put my life in the place where He can give me what He desires to give me, or I will disobey Him and put my life in the place where He cannot give me the good that He desires to give me.

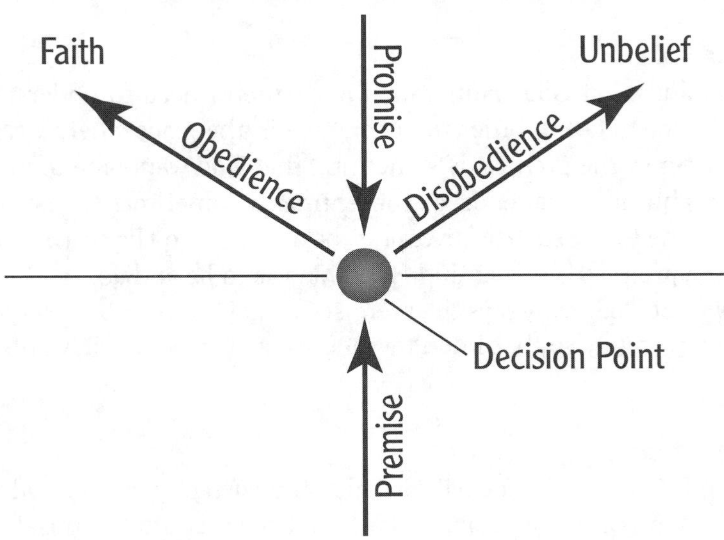

Once again, my heavenly Father is a perfect parent. Good parents don't reward their child for disobedient behavior. That would just encourage more disobedience in the child. Good parents want their children to obey them because it is the best thing for the child. When the child lives in obedience to the parent, then all the good things the parent desires to give the child can flow freely.

Faith is, in essence, obeying the premise in order to receive the promise. The Father says, "Do this (because I know it is best for you) and I will do this." Am I willing to take Him at His word and obey the premise? When I do, that is what the Bible calls faith. Faith is obedience to the premises that God establishes for His promises.

So, for me to act in faith I must do three things:

Know the Promise

I must first know what God has promised to do. In other words, "What does His Word mean?" This means when I come to the Bible, His Word, I must be careful that I don't try to make it say something that it doesn't say. In other words, I must do as Paul admonished Timothy to do:

Be diligent to present yourself approved to God as a workman who does not need to be ashamed, accurately handling the word of truth. (2 Timothy 2:15)

We must always be careful that we don't read a meaning into Scripture that we *want* it to have. What God means is all that matters. So, every promise, every passage, must be interpreted in light of its immediate context, as well as the context of the entirety of Scripture, to make sure we understand what God is saying in His Word.

Know the Premise

Once I understand what God wants me to have, then I need to understand what He wants me to be (or to do) in order to put my life in the place where I can access His promise. Sometimes the premise is something that God wants me to be. An internal attitude such as humility, patience, or contentment. Sometimes the premise is something He wants me to do, such as give, pray, be a witness to His truth, and on and on. Sometimes, the premise is something He wants me to be and do. In each situation, I want to know what God really says the premise is. Again, I must be careful to interpret the Scripture accurately so that I don't wrongly construe what He wants me to be or do.

Practice the Premise

Once I have rightly understood God's promise and correctly interpreted the premise, then the next step is for me to act in faith and practice the premise! Get into the wheelbarrow and do what He has said for me to do! If He has said, "Give!" then I must give. If He says I must pray, then I must pray. If He says I must allow Him to renew my mind, then I must allow Him to renew my mind. If He says I must live a sexually pure life, then I must live a sexually pure life. If He says I must seek first His kingdom, then I must seek first His kingdom.

Wait on the Promise

This is so important. I must be willing to continue to act in faith (i.e., practice the premise) until God's timing is right for me to receive the promise. His timing is not the same as my timing. My timing is "right now!" His timing is "when the time is right." Sometimes He may allow me to practice the premise for a long time before He delivers the promise. If I take Him at His word and trust Him, then I will be willing to wait. If I am only trying to manipulate Him for my own purposes, I will probably give up when I don't receive the promise immediately.

Joseph in the Old Testament exemplifies this truth. His story is told in Genesis 37–50. At the age of seventeen Joseph was sold by his brothers into slavery because they were jealous of him. Over the next thirteen years, Joseph was not only a slave but falsely accused by Potiphar's wife, thrown in prison, and taken advantage of by people he helped while in prison. For thirteen years he endured all of this. However, Joseph eventually arrived where God intended him to be—in a position of power in Egypt as the right-hand man to Pharaoh. How did Joseph go through all of that seemingly unending trouble and eventually assume the position he did? Because through it all, Joseph practiced the premise. He stayed faithful to God. He didn't compromise his character. In God's time, Joseph received the stature God promised him.

The essence of this step is to "humbly ask God to remove our character defects." Is this something that He desires to do? I believe it is. All of the Christian life is about being changed by Christ. In fact, it is about becoming "like Christ."

> *For those whom He foreknew, He also predestined to become conformed to the image of His Son . . . (Romans 8:29a)*

> *And do not be conformed to this world but be transformed by the renewing of your mind . . . (Romans 12:2a)*

We could go on and on pointing out that it is the Father's will to bring change in our lives. That's His promise to us.

Well, what is the premise? If you have been doing your work seriously in the first five steps, you have already begun practicing some important parts of the premise.

You Admit that you are powerless. You Believe the truth. You have begun searching out those lies that are at the base of many of the un-Christlike attitudes and behaviors that have caused you problems. You Commit to Christ. If you did the third step correctly, there should be no question that you are the Father's child through faith in Jesus Christ.

You have Discovered responsibility in your fearless and searching moral inventory. You have Exposed the secret by confessing to yourself, God, and one other person. My point is that you have already begun to practice the premises for life change that the Father desires to bring in your life.

There will be more to come as we move further through this process and as you learn what they are you will begin to practice them. All of these things are putting your life in the place where God can give you what He wants to give you—life change.

So what might this prayer look and sound like? It should be very specific, don't you think? Instead of a general, "one size fits all" kind of prayer, it should name the specific shortcomings and the specific character defects that you are asking Him to remove.

For instance, where I have blamed others in the past, I want to take responsibility. Where I have lied and deceived, I'm asking Him to make me a person of integrity. A truthful person. Where I have in the past isolated from others, I want to "press into" others. Where I have had resentment, I want to forgive. Where I have powered up to control others, I want to power down. Where I have always been a taker, I want Him to make me a giver. We could go on and on, couldn't we?

Bizarro World

In an episode of the hugely successful sitcom, *Seinfeld,* Jerry and his friends encounter their bizarro counterparts. Where Jerry is fickle, his bizarro Jerry is steady. Where Kramer is crazy, his bizarro opposite is calm and collected. Where George is flighty and insecure, bizarro George is collected and secure. You get the idea. All the things they should be are reflected in their bizarro opposite.

In this step we are in essence asking God to change us into our bizarro double. We know that He desires to make those changes, don't we? That's His promise. He wants us to be more like Jesus. Jesus is the ultimate expression of our bizarro self! He desires for us to move beyond our defects that cause Him, ourselves, and others, pain. That's His promise. So, what is the premise?

I need to look at my bizarro double, see the behavior that he/she demonstrates, and imitate it. When I do, I will be acting in the way God has told me to act—practicing the premise. If I struggle with selfishness, then I need to act as a generous person would act. Find ways to give. If I am prone to isolate myself from people, then I must find ways to "press into" people and relationships. If there are certain people I am jealous of, then I need to find ways to love, serve, and encourage them, rather than envy them. In other words, acting as a person who had no jealousy would act. Whatever the character defect is, I must step out of my normal behavior as an act of faith and begin to demonstrate the opposite. That is my part. Obey God. His part, in turn, will be to renew my mind and change me from the inside out as I choose to honor Him and obey Him.

If Nothing Changes . . .

One of the truths of the universe is, "If nothing changes, nothing changes." Another way of saying this is, "You can't have change without change." If we keep doing the same thing over and over, we will continue to get the same results. Day after day, year after year, relationship after relationship, pain after more pain, blah, blah, blah. Remember the Valley of Despair illustration in step B, Believe the Truth?

In this application, "where I am" is my character defect. "Where I want to be" is more like Christ. To get there, I must cross the valley of despair. It feels awkward, out of my norm, fake, not like me. It feels that way because it's all of those things . . . for a while. If disobedience to God is the norm in an area of your life, then to begin living obediently will be uncomfortable. When jealousy is what I am accustomed to, then acting the opposite of jealousy will be uncomfortable. When isolation and separation from people is my norm, it feels uncomfortable to move toward people.

The Chicken or the Egg?

It's age-old question, isn't it? Which comes first? Well, which does comes first? Obedience or transformation? Does God change me and then I obey, or do I obey and then God changes me? The answer is both! When I place my trust in Christ as Savior, as we discussed in the third step, I become a new creation in Christ. The character of Christ is placed within me. Not only that, but the Holy Spirit of God dwells permanently within me to guide me, empower me, and encourage me. I am saved from the eternal penalty for my sin. Therefore, I am changed and I am changing. The chicken and the egg!

The entirety of the Christian life is about releasing the character of Christ that has been in me from the point of my salvation. It's the epic battle between the flesh and the Spirit, spoken of in Romans 7. How is this battle won in any area of my life? When I choose to begin acting upon fact (faith)—not feeling.

Another way of asking the question is, "Which comes first, fact or feeling?" Must I *feel* like obeying before I obey? Or must I act upon the fact of God's premises and allow feelings to follow? The second option is what the Scripture teaches. I must obey because obedience is right whether I feel like it or not. What is the engine of the train? Fact or feeling? The following graphic illustrates the question.

The engine of the train is the *fact* of the obedience God asks of me. The caboose is the *feeling* of obedience. Which drives the train? Fact or feeling? Engine or caboose? The truth is, often we try to let the caboose drive the train, even though the caboose doesn't have an engine! It has no power to move the train forward. Therefore, when we live our lives according to feeling we stay stuck right where we are, dead on the track. Stranded. Fact is the only one of the two that has any power. Fact is the engine that can drive the train and get the train moving forward in a positive direction.

The middle car is *faith*. Faith connects fact and feeling. I must "take God at His word" that if I act according to fact then eventually real change will happen within me and the feeling will follow. I have to trust (faith) that if I act upon the premise (fact) God is going to honor His promise (feeling) and when I come out of the valley, I will want to obey, feel like obeying, and enjoy the benefits of obedience.

Principle: Begin to talk to yourself and stop listening to yourself.

When you are listening to yourself you are hearing your feelings. As long as you listen, your feelings will continue to drive your behavior. When your feelings begin to talk, you have to stop listening and begin speaking. Speak the truth to yourself. The facts. What God says about the situation, behavior, or circumstance. If you want the engine to begin driving the train you have to stop listening to feeling and speak the truth to yourself.

Prepare Your Defect List

As you prepare the list of defects that you are specifically going to ask God to remove, you need to understand how this works. First, identify the defect—selfishness, jealousy, laziness, untrustworthiness, and the like. Then, identify the promise of what God wants you to become. This will be the opposite of the defect that you listed. Finally, identify the premise. Specific actions, with specific people, that you need to take to counter the defect. For instance, I am jealous of Suzie because she is so talented. The *promise* is that God wants me to be an encourager of others. The *premise* is that I will specifically build Suzie up to other people and find ways to encourage her. I will tell her how her voice blesses me when I hear her sing. I will write her a card and encourage her to continue to use her talent to bring honor to God. These are things a "non-jealous" person would do!

What are the specific character defects you want God to change? List the defect and then list what you would like to look like.

The defect I ask God to remove ________________________________

The Promise: What He wants me to be like. Bizarro me! Opposite of defect ________

____

The Premise: What must I begin to do? ____________________________

The defect I ask God to remove ________________________________

The Promise: What He wants me to be like. Bizarro me! Opposite of defect ________

____

The Premise: What must I begin to do?__________________________________

The defect I ask God to remove ______________________________________

The Promise: What He wants me to be like. Bizarro me! Opposite of defect ________

____

The Premise: What must I begin to do? __________________________________

The defect I ask God to remove ______________________________________

The Promise: What He wants me to be like. Bizarro me! Opposite of defect ________

____

The Premise: What must I begin to do? __________________________________

Make the Ask

Now it's time to "make the ask!" Ask God, ask Him humbly, ask Him with the faith that you have already begun to demonstrate. Will it all be over when you ask God to do this? No, it won't. It will come in His time, not your time. But one thing is certain. If you continue in the premise, He will keep His promise.

> Take your list of defects and go to Him in prayer and humbly ask Him to remove them.
>
> Ask Him for the power to live the premise to counter each defect.
>
> Don't forget to thank him in advance for the change he is going to bring.

What is the most important thing you have learned in this step?________________

____

What do you plan to do in your marriage this week as a result of this step? ________

____

TABLE TALK

What is the most important thing about you that relates to this chapter that you are going to share with your spouse this week?

____

____

____

____

JOURNAL

11

“G”—Go Get Right

“We made a list of all the persons we had harmed and became willing to make amends to them all. We made direct amends to such people wherever possible, except where to do so would injure them or others.”

THE PROBLEM OF “G”

So far in the process, we have been doing some personal house cleaning. We had messed up our house. We have acknowledged that and have been taking steps to clean up the house. Beginning with this step, we start doing some “social” house cleaning. We have not only messed up our house, but we have dirtied up some other people’s houses with our attitudes and our actions. Now we want to make that right.

The challenge of “G” comes in two parts. The first part is our willingness to take full responsibility. It’s one thing to admit our responsibility to ourselves, God, and one other person, as we did in the previous step. It’s another thing altogether to be willing to go to the person we have wronged and admit our responsibility to him or her. Even the thought of that perhaps causes a lump in the throat or a turning of the stomach. However, this is the true expression of humility and a willingness to fully own our part in broken relationships, attitudes, and behaviors that have been destructive to us and others.

This is the goal and the challenge at the same time. In other words, if we take full responsibility by acting on this step, then we have overcome the challenge and we have achieved the goal, no matter how the other person responds. We have no control over their response. We can take no responsibility for their response. We only have control over what we do and the responsibility we take. Therefore, we approach this step without any expectations of what their response might be, either positive or negative. If the other person receives us and welcomes us, that is a blessing. If the person remains angry, bitter, and resentful, and completely rejects us, that is his or her response, and the person is responsible for that.

That's the second part of the challenge of this step. We have to overcome our expectations. We may sit and dream about what their response might be. In a perfect world and in the vision of our dreams, we may see them crying, throwing their arms around us and forgiving us, and then taking responsibility for anything they might have done to us. That makes sweet dreams, and sometimes it might even happen, but we must do away with that expectation. Clean the slate. Why? Because if that is what we are expecting, and it doesn't happen, then we have defeated the purpose of this step. This step is about us, not them. This step is about my responsibility, not theirs. This step is about my humility, not their pride. If I genuinely and humbly accomplish this step, I can walk away knowing I have done my part, all I could do, regardless of how they responded. Any other expectation will set me up for disappointment and failure.

> *If possible, so far as it depends upon you, be at peace with all men. (Romans 12:18)*

As the old television series, *Mission Impossible,* used to say, "This is your mission, should you choose to accept it." To achieve life change, to accept full responsibility for my actions, I must accept it.

Are you ready to accept full responsibility? ____________________ Why or why not?

____

____

Is there one person who comes to mind immediately? ________________________

If so, what concerns you about going to this person?__________________________

____

____

____

THE PROCESS OF "G"

Once again, this step first addresses your wants. You must want to take full responsibility. You must want to be free of the guilt and shame you have carried because of harmful attitudes and actions on your part toward others. In this step we are in essence, going to others, confessing our wrong to them, accepting responsibility for those wrongs, and asking their forgiveness. Whether they extend that forgiveness or not is up to them and, as we have said, not our responsibility.

However, before we can in good conscience ask for their forgiveness, we have to deal with another subject. What about those who have wronged us and we are still harboring unforgiveness? If we come to God and ask His forgiveness for our wrongdoings through Jesus Christ, then we take on the responsibility of giving forgiveness to others in the same way we have received it. This truth is taught all through the Word of God.

And forgive us our debts, as we also have forgiven our debtors. (Matthew 6:12)

As I stated in the emotional/spiritual principle discussion, if I pray this way I am effectively asking God to limit my experience of His forgiveness to the level that I have been willing to forgive others.

Then Peter came and said to Him, "Lord, how often shall my brother sin against me and I forgive him? Up to seven times? Jesus said to him, "I do not say to you up to seven times, but up to seventy times seven." (Matthew 18:21–22)

Obviously, the idea is that I must keep on forgiving just as God has forgiven me. Since this is true, before I can go and ask forgiveness from others, I must do something about the unforgiveness I am harboring in my own heart. It's the essence of hypocrisy to receive forgiveness from God, ask it from those whom I have wronged, and yet withhold it from those who have wronged me.

However, because there are so many misconceptions about forgiveness, and these hinder our ability to practice it, we need to think about what forgiveness is, what it isn't, and how we can practice it. Then we will come to how we can fulfill this specific step of making amends.

Can you think of anyone right now that you are harboring unforgiveness toward?

What did they do to you? ____

____

____

The Forgiveness I Extend to Others

Much of the following discussion has appeared previously in my book, *Refuge*. However, it is so germane to having a full understanding of this step, I feel it necessary to repeat it here in this context.

Why Should I Forgive?

Good question. It ranks right up there with questions like, "Why should I breathe?" "Why should I eat?" "Why should I drink water?" Because if I don't, I'll die! Simple enough. Forgiveness is as necessary to emotional and spiritual health as breathing, eating, and drinking water are to physical health and life! I'll die if I don't breathe, eat, or drink. I'll die from the inside out if I don't forgive.

Now that I have your attention, let me give three very practical reasons why we must forgive. This is just information and information by itself never changes anything. But having good information can sometimes be a catalyst that launches us into good behavior. It's the behavior of forgiveness we are shooting for, not just the information; but we do need to begin with the right information.

The Grace Reason

There is a principle in Scripture that appears over and over that goes like this, "Forgive just as you have been forgiven." Jesus told a parable in Matthew 18 that is built upon this principle. It's a story about a certain king who had a servant who owed him a huge sum of money. In fact, the amount was so large that the servant would never have been able to pay it all back. He would have gone to his death indebted to the king. The king, out of kindness and compassion for the servant, forgave the debt. In its entirety! In total. Wiped the ledger clean. You can imagine the joy of the servant! I can just see him skipping out of the king's presence shouting, "Yea! That's what I'm talking about!" But then, on his way out, he came across a fellow servant who owed him a few measly bucks. Nothing in comparison with the debt he had owed the king. But he said to his fellow servant, "Pay up!" The fellow servant promised to pay but pled for more time. The first servant refused! He said, "Pay me right now or I will have you thrown in prison!" And, that's exactly what he did to the other servant.

Word got back to the king about what had transpired between the two servants. The king was hacked to the limit. He called the first servant back in and called him a wicked servant. He said, "I forgave you freely, and you should also be willing to freely forgive." Then the king had him thrown in prison. The point the king (and Jesus) was making is, "How could you withhold forgiveness from others when you have been forgiven so much?" Great question. How could I? It doesn't make any sense, does it?

When my seventy-three-year-old friend, whom I baptized on his seventy-third birthday, told me there were people he didn't think he could ever forgive, I had a similar rejoinder for him. I said, "Gordon, did God forgive you for thumbing your nose at him for seventy-two years?" He said, "Yes, He did." I replied, "Then, you can forgive anyone of anything they might have done to you." The grace I have received demands that I extend grace to others. I don't say that to heap guilt or shame upon anyone for their struggle to forgive. I understand the struggle. I have been there. I make the statement as an encouragement to keep each one of us in touch with the magnitude of the forgiveness we have received. I need to keep my eyes upon the debt that I have been freely forgiven of by the grace of God through Jesus. The more in touch I am with that grace, the more I will be willing to keep moving forward and extending forgiveness to those who have wronged me.

What is the level of grace you have received from God?

____

____

____

____

The Guilt Reason

I don't know about you, but I haven't stopped needing forgiveness. I have needed forgiveness from God in the past, and I'm going to need it in the future. The knowledge that I will have to come to Him again (before this day is closed) for forgiveness provides me with strong incentive to forgive those who have wronged me!

I'm reminded of the story of the old prospector who rode his mule into town and tied him to a hitching post. Then he went into the saloon. A drunken cowboy thought he'd have some fun with the old guy, so he pulled out his six-shooter and said, "Old man, did you ever dance the jig?" "Nope," replied the prospector. So, the cowboy began to shoot at the old man's feet causing him to hop from foot to foot, dancing the jig. When the cowboy ran out of bullets the prospector turned and walked out the saloon door. In a little while, the cowboy stumbled out that same door. When he looked up, he was staring right into the business end of a double-barreled shotgun in the old prospector's hands. He said to the cowboy, "Cowboy, did you ever kiss a mule?" To which the cowboy replied, "Nope, but I always wanted to!"

He suddenly had a strong incentive to kiss a mule! He couldn't wait to kiss a mule! It became his passion in life to kiss a mule! When I look at the likelihood that I am going to have to come to the heavenly Father to confess my own infractions against Him, as well as against others, it gives me strong incentive to forgive! I want to be able to walk in the freshness and freedom of His forgiveness. Therefore, I need to be willing to extend it to others. I have a strong incentive to forgive.

Do you anticipate having to come to the Father in the future for grace?

____

____

____

____

What do you need to do to be able to freely ask Him for forgiveness without hypocrisy?

____

____

____

____

The Grief Reason

The truth is, when I refuse to offer forgiveness it causes me all kinds of grief. Why is it that we would ever want to withhold forgiveness from someone else? There's only one reason really. We think that by withholding forgiveness, we can somehow make them pay or cause them grief for what they did to us. We feel they owe us something, and we want to collect on the debt! We want our pound of flesh.

The problem is that it doesn't work that way. We say something like this, "You owe me for what you did to me." Then we follow it up with, "I'll pay you back!" Did you get that contradiction? You owe me, but I'm the one who is going to pay back? It isn't really a contradiction because that is exactly what happens when I hold onto unforgiveness. I become the debtor! I become the one who really pays. Every time I withhold forgiveness, I write an emotional and spiritual I.O.U. I go deeper and deeper in debt to the person I refuse to forgive! Ultimately, the one who pays the price for unforgiveness is not the offender, but the one who has been offended. The pain then gets doubled. Not only do I have the pain from the original offense against me, but now it's compounded by the pain that results from my unwillingness to forgive. I just keep digging my dark hole of pain deeper and deeper. I collect nothing. I lose every time. Hebrews 12:15 says, "See to it that no one comes short of the grace of God; that no *root of bitterness* springing up causes trouble, and by it many be defiled." Every time I refuse to forgive, a seed is dropped into the soil of my spirit. A bitterness seed. I can choose to forgive my offender and crush that seed before it can germinate, or I can make another choice. I can choose not to forgive. When I make that choice, the seed germinates, sprouts, and grows. Eventually, the roots of that bitterness dive deep inside and wrap themselves around my heart. Then the toxins of bitterness pour into my spirit. There are two things the passage says the root of bitterness does. It causes trouble and it defiles.

My unwillingness to forgive causes me trouble. It compounds the trouble of the original offense against me, and then it causes me trouble of its own. It's double trouble. But it also defiles. The word used here has the idea of "contamination" or "pollution." Unforgiveness and bitterness make my life a toxic waste dump! Nothing grows in toxic waste. The poison permeates and affects every area of my life. It drains all of my joy. It sickens my relationships. Medical science tells us that over a prolonged period of time, the stress of bitterness even has negative effects on my body! It sucks all the nutrients out of the soil of my life and nothing good can grow, emotionally, spiritually, or physically.

Someone has said, "Holding onto bitterness is like drinking poison and waiting for the other person to die." They don't die, I do. All unforgiveness does is cause me more grief. It allows the person who has already hurt me to continue to hurt me. The only way to stop the hurt is to forgive.

How has withholding forgiveness affected you (i.e., what impact has it made)?

____

____

____

____

Has it made you feel proud of yourself?

____

____

____

____

____

Has it made you feel powerful?

____

____

____

____

Has it made you feel like you were getting some payback?

____

____

____

____

Myths about Forgiveness

Our world is filled with myths. There is the myth of Bigfoot. It makes great campfire talk on a starry night, but come on! Nobody really believes this stuff, do they? Some people do. There is the myth of the Loch Ness monster in Scotland. For decades, scientists from around the world have spent hundreds of thousands of dollars trying to verify the existence of Nessie (as the locals affectionately call it.) Does anyone really believe this stuff? Evidently, some still do. Almost on a daily basis, I get emails about things and I say, "That can't really be true." Often it isn't. There is even a website devoted to debunking these urban legends and myths. In spite of that, I still find people who believe them. I guess they just want to.

There are also myths about forgiveness that some people still believe. These myths aren't as harmless as holding onto the belief in a Sasquatch,or a Loch Ness monster. Myths about forgiveness cause a great deal of damage and sometimes keep people from even attempting to forgive! These myths have to be dispelled from our minds before we can move into an understanding of what forgiveness really is. There are certainly more, but I want to point out four of the most damaging myths about forgiveness.

Myth #1: Forgiveness Can Be Conditional

Sometimes people approach forgiveness as if it was a bargaining process. My wife and I recently visited New York City. We spent a morning walking up and down the streets of

SoHo in Manhattan. On the southern border of SoHo is an area known as Chinatown. All up and down the street there are vendors selling their wares. It's crowded, it's loud, and it's a blast! I love the energy of the place. What really makes it so much fun is that you never pay the asking price, at least not if you are smart. How great is that? Every purchase is preceded by a friendly (usually friendly, at least) haggling session. You go back and forth with the vendor bargaining over the price. At the end, hopefully you get what you wanted at a price you feel good about, and the vendor makes a sale at a profit he can live with. Vendors always get their profit or they don't make the deal. Forgiveness isn't anything like that. Forgiveness isn't a bargaining process.

We can't come to forgiveness and say, "I'll forgive you if . . ." There are no "ifs" in forgiveness, just as there is no crying in baseball! You either forgive or you don't. For forgiveness to be real, and effective, it must be an unconditional, unilateral decision that we make regardless of the other person's response. Conditional forgiveness is no forgiveness at all.

Does the person need to deserve forgiveness before I give it?

____

____

____

____

Why?

____

____

____

____

Myth #2: If I Forgive, That Will Minimize the Wrong That Was Done

Sometimes we withhold forgiveness because we believe if we forgive it will minimize the other person's offense. We feel that forgiveness means writing off the enormity of the wrong that has been perpetrated against us. Nothing could be further from the truth. In fact, the opposite is true. To truly forgive, we must first fully acknowledge the enormity of the wrong. If it wasn't a big deal to begin with, it wouldn't warrant forgiveness. The fact that we have to forgive illustrates that it was a big deal! Forgiveness doesn't negate that. If someone has wronged you, then the hurt is real and the resulting consequences may have been devastating! Forgiveness doesn't mean you have to minimize or deny the truth of that. Fully accept it. Fully acknowledge the pain and the hurt it has caused you. Then, quickly begin the process of forgiving.

In October 2006, an incredible tragedy took place in an Amish community of Pennsylvania. A man came into their one-room schoolhouse and took young children hostage. He released the teacher and all of the boys, but kept the girls. Then he lined them up against a blackboard and shot ten of them, execution style, before turning the gun on himself. Five of the girls died immediately. Days later, a sixth died of her injuries. Four others went to the hospital in critical or serious condition. The nation was astounded to hear the Amish community immediately speak about forgiveness. They didn't just speak about it—they offered it. Not only to the thirty-two-year-old man who had terrorized and murdered their daughters, but also to the man's wife and family. They reached out to her in recognition of the pain she was also feeling. They invited her to the funerals, according to Amish custom. America was astounded at the response of these simple people who demonstrated a profound faith in God. Most people can't even begin to understand it. To the Amish, there was never a question about what they would do. Their offer of forgiveness in no way minimized the horror of what had happened. They were grieving deeply as anyone would in that kind of situation. But they understood that part of their healing was their forgiveness.

Has anyone ever done something to you that was so bad you thought it would never be possible to forgive them? If so, what?

____

____

Has anything like that happened in your marriage? What?

____

____

____

____

____

Is it important for you to forgive that?

____

____

____

____

Myth #3: Forgiveness Means the Relationship Must Be Reconciled

Wrong. Forgiveness and reconciliation are two separate issues. Sometimes both can happen, sometimes they can't. For reconciliation to happen, forgiveness is a must. On the other hand, reconciliation is not a must for forgiveness to happen. Reconciliation requires that both parties participate. Forgiveness requires only the participation of the one who was wronged. Forgiveness can be a unilateral act.

Sometimes, reconciliation is not even possible. The person might no longer be living. Perhaps their whereabouts are unknown. They may not want anything to do with you! If reconciliation was required, you could never forgive. You'd be stuck! Often, the other person is unwilling to admit their wrong and ask for forgiveness. But you can still forgive! Forgiveness requires only your action.

Is there someone you need to forgive with whom reconciliation is not even possible?

Who? ______________________________ Why is it not possible?

____

____

Myth #4: If I Forgive I Have to Forget

Perhaps you have heard someone say, "You have to forgive and forget." This is one of the most damaging platitudes that has ever been perpetrated by well-meaning people. It sounds so good on its face. It even sounds very spiritual (we love spiritual platitudes, don't we?), because the Bible says when God forgives He "remembers it no more." Does that mean the God who knows all things actually forgets? I don't think so. What it means is, He holds it against us no more. He puts it away!

The truth is, the best way to remember something is to try to forget it! Try to forget something and it will be all you think about! Try it sometime. When you come into the house next time, put your car keys down and tell yourself you are going to concentrate on forgetting where you put them. Concentrate on it. Work at it! I'm going to forget that I put them on the table next to the sofa. You won't even have to look for them the next morning. Their location will be burned into your memory.

There are some things that are so hurtful and damaging, they are impossible to forget. It isn't the remembering that is the problem anyway. The problem is the power the memory has over you. The goal of forgiveness is not to be released from the memory. The goal is to be released from the power the memory has over you.

So, what forgiveness accomplishes is not forgetfulness, but release. Forgiveness allows me to dig up the root of bitterness that has caused me so much trouble and defiled my life and be set free from it. I still have the memory, but the memory no longer has me. I am released from its power.

What Forgiveness Is Not

1. Forgiveness Is Not Enabling

We are called to forgive, but we are not called to enable a person to continue the bad behavior for which we have forgiven them. For instance, if a family member has stolen a credit card of mine and run up a huge bill, I have to forgive him. But that doesn't mean that I have to make my credit cards available to him again. That would be enabling continued destructive behavior.

2. Forgiveness Is Not Rescuing

We rescue people when we keep them from experiencing the consequences of the behavior for which we have forgiven them. Rescuing is not helpful because most often it is those very consequences that bring the person to a realization of their need to change. For instance, if I have taught my children to respect the property of others, yet my child vandalizes and destroys someone else's property, what must I do? I must forgive my child. But forgiveness does not mean that I help my child to get off easy or escape the consequences. The best thing for the child to do would be to face the consequences, get a job, make reparations, and do whatever the law demanded. Forgiving the child does not mean rescuing the child.

3. Forgiveness Is Not Risking

Forgiveness never requires that we knowingly put ourselves at risk of the person perpetrating hurt and pain upon us again. For instance, if we have been abused by a family member or significant person in our life, what should we do? Forgive. But forgiveness does not mean we have to put ourselves at risk for further abuse. Healthy boundaries always need to be maintained. Forgiveness does not mean that we have to make ourselves available for another person to abuse or harm us.

What Forgiveness Is

Once the myths are dispelled, we can focus on what forgiveness is and how to accomplish it. Our goal in the Hospital Church is to help hurting people understand that anyone can forgive anyone for anything! In fact, the greater the wrong, the more necessary forgiveness becomes. As the wrongs increase, so also the damaging effects of unforgiveness increase. The need to forgive grows in proportion to the difficulty of the forgiveness. The greater the wrong, the more difficult it is to forgive, but also the more important forgiveness becomes. Someone may say, "I could never forgive that person. What they did to me was so bad that I could never forgive." We will say, "the horrible nature of what they did to you makes it that much more imperative that you forgive." So, what do we tell people who come to the Hospital Church about forgiveness? We tell them some truths about forgiveness. Here are three of them.

Truth #1: Forgiveness Is an Act of the Will

It's a fact that when the Bible speaks about forgiveness, it speaks about it as a command. Forgiveness isn't a nice suggestion. It's a divine imperative. Jesus said, "Forgive as you have been forgiven." That's a command. Commands are directed at the will, not the emotions. You can't command true emotions. When someone is hurting, it does no good to command, "Feel better!" Emotions can't be commanded. Therefore, forgiveness has to be an act of the will that may or may not involve the emotions. Forgiveness won't always involve warm fuzzy feelings. Sometimes warm feelings might happen, but the forgiveness and the emotion are completely separate. For example, if someone has physically or sexually abused you, it may not only be unreasonable, but even abusive, to expect you to ever have warm fuzzy feelings toward that person—particularly if the perpetrator never expresses any remorse or admits any wrongdoing. However, that does not prevent us from extending forgiveness. Forgiveness is an act of the will, not the emotions. It's a decision we make. A choice.

Truth #2: Forgiveness Is an Act of Release

In the Bible, the word that is translated "forgiveness" literally means "to release." Forgiveness is a release. I actually release the person from my debt. We still use the word this way sometimes when we speak of a debt. We release the person. We "forgive" the debt. In forgiveness, I declare, "You owe me nothing." There is nothing that I expect to get from you, so I release you. As has already been stated, when we withhold forgiveness, it's most often because we don't want to release the person from our debt. We believe there is something we can get from the one who has wronged us. We want him/her to pay up. Of course, what happens is that we are held captive by our own unforgiveness. It ends up being us that pays, not the person who wronged us. The irony of forgiveness is that when I forgive, when I release the person, it's really me that is released.

On a Saturday night, October 7, 2006, I was sitting at our kitchen table working on the final touches of my notes for my message on Sunday morning. The television was on and tuned into the program *Dateline NBC*. I could hear the interviewer speaking with the brother of one of the girls who had been killed in the Columbine High School rampage of 1999. His name was Craig Scott, and his sister, Rachel, was one of the victims. He spoke about how his anger and rage had lasted for years after the shooting. After awhile he began to speak about the time when he realized he had to forgive his sister's killer or it was going to kill him. Then he made the statement that made me stop what I was doing and pick up my pen. He said, "Forgiveness is like setting a prisoner free, then finding out that the prisoner was you." Wow! He spoke with such calm and peace I knew for certain those were not just words. He had experienced that release personally.

What does it mean when we release someone who has wronged us? This is what we tell people to picture. Picture yourself turning them over to God. You are saying if there is anything that needs to be collected, you will leave it to God to collect it! Guess what? He will do a much better job of collecting whatever needs to be collected than you or I could ever do.

Romans 12:19 says, "Never take your own revenge, beloved, but leave room for the wrath of God, for it is written, 'Vengeance is mine, I will repay,' says the Lord."

If collection needs to be made, it's God's job to do it. I turn the person over to Him. Before the "act" of forgiveness can happen, there must first be an "attitude" of forgiveness. It's the "attitude" of forgiveness that sets me free. It's the "act" of forgiveness that sets the other person free. In other words, when I cross the line in my heart that says, "I do want to forgive," I have moved into the attitude of forgiveness. I begin to be released. It's then a small step to the actual "act" of forgiveness. Coming to the attitude of forgiveness is usually much more difficult, and takes more time, than the actual act of forgiveness itself.

Truth #3: Forgiveness Is an Act of Faith

This fact flows out of the one just discussed. If we are going to release to God the person who wronged us, then we have to trust in the character of God. We must trust that what He has told us about the need to forgive is true. We have to trust that He will deal with the person we release in a just way. That's scary, isn't it? It means I must not only release the person, but I must release control of the situation and turn it over to God.

In fact, I have discovered that sometimes before the issue of forgiveness can be addressed effectively, the subject of the character of God must be dealt with. Usually, the first step of forgiveness is to unpack the baggage and clear up the confusion about the character and nature of God! He is just. He is faithful. His character is intact, and He can be trusted.

From the last step, what is faith?

___

___

___

___

That means that when I forgive someone what must I trust God to do?

___

___

___

___

How Forgiveness Happens

What I want to suggest here is not a formula. There is no formula for forgiveness. Forgiveness, like most things, is a process. Each individual has to work through that process on his or her own. It may happen differently for you than it does for me. What matters isn't how it happens, but that it happens. I heard someone say once, "If you're getting it done, I like the way you're doing it!" That's what we would say to someone in the Hospital Church who is working through his or her process of forgiveness. If you're getting it done, I like the way you're doing it.

Beware of people who tell you how to forgive. What worked in his/her life may or may not work for you. We are all in danger of codifying what has happened for us, and telling others that is how it must happen for them. A principle I discovered years ago became a key to unlocking many of the questions I had about how much of the Scripture applied to me today. Two key words: descriptive and prescriptive. In other words, there are two kinds of Scripture. There is Scripture that describes how God worked in a certain situation, at a certain time, and with a certain person. That doesn't mean He works that way all the time. For example, in Acts 5, the story of Ananias and Sapphira is told. The essence of the story is that they sold some land and pretended to give it all for the benefit of the early church. However, they held some back for themselves secretly. They wanted to be perceived as being more generous than they were. For that act of deception, the Scripture says God struck them down and they died. Obviously, that Scripture is descriptive in nature. It's describing how God worked in that situation. It certainly isn't saying that is how He always works. If it were, then most of us would already be dead! There are principles that can be gleaned from the event, but it can't be used as an illustration of how God always works. It's descriptive in nature.

The other is prescriptive Scripture. Prescriptive Scripture states a universal principle that applies to all people, in all situations, at all times. For instance, Galatians 6:7 states the principle that whatever a man sows is what he will reap. That's prescriptive. It's always true. It may not happen immediately; it takes time for a crop to come in. It may not happen in the way we expect it to, but it is prescriptive. It's always true. The kind of seed you plant will determine the harvest that comes in.

So, how does all of this apply in the area of forgiveness? Well, the Scripture tells us that we are to forgive. That's prescriptive. It's a command of God, given for our own good. But there is no prescription about *how* we are to forgive. There is no formula in Scripture that prescribes a step-by-step process that must be followed. We can find principles in Scripture that will help and guide us, and that can be applied in the area of forgiveness, but there is no formula given for forgiveness. Therefore, each one of us must negotiate this process for ourselves under the guidance of the Spirit of God.

Rather than give a formula for forgiveness, it's better to suggest principles that, when applied, can help us in the process. I want to mention four of them that we in the Hospital Church try to help people understand. I pray they will help you to successfully negotiate the turbulent waters of forgiveness, as well as help others.

Principle #1: Seek to Understand

You can never go wrong by seeking to understand the pain and hurt the other person has experienced. Someone has said, "We hurt others out of our own hurt." That is true. It doesn't excuse the hurt that we cause others, or that others have caused us, but it's never wrong to seek to understand. Remember, someone else is probably going to have to forgive you for hurt you have caused him or her. Would you like for them to attempt to understand what hurt and pain inside of you contributed to your hurtful behavior? Probably. Seeking to understand is always a good thing.

Think of one person that you need to forgive. What can you understand about them that explains (not excuses) their actions?

____

____

____

____

Principle #2: Always Remember the Forgiveness You Have Received

The truth is that there is no forgiveness I could ever be called upon to give to another person that could come near to matching the forgiveness I have received in Christ. When Jesus was hanging on the cross, He prayed, "Father, forgive them for they do not know what they are doing." Jesus wasn't speaking only about those who physically nailed Him to the cross. He was speaking of me. I crucified Jesus. It was for my sin that He died. On the cross, Jesus paid the debt of my sin that I might be forgiven by the Father freely, fully, and finally. He closed the book on the eternal penalty for my sin. What a great act of forgiveness!

The enormity of that truth is almost more than I can wrap my limited understanding around. It always helps to keep that in front of me. About the time I begin to think something is just too much for me to forgive, all I have to do is go back to the cross. It helps me to keep it all in perspective. In the Hospital Church, we are careful to keep the cross in full view for people. Every one of us must constantly go back to the cross and connect again with the magnitude of what happened there on our behalf. That isn't to make us feel guilty for the struggle we have in forgiving those who have hurt us. Be careful you don't go there. He understands that struggle. Just let it be a reminder and an encouragement to continue to process. However long that process takes.

Principle #3: Focus on One Person, One Hurt at a Time

It could be that over the course of life you have accumulated a long list of people who have wounded and hurt you. If that is the case, then the forgiveness process can look so massive that you just may give up before you even begin. It would be tragic for that to happen.

If you have a long list of hurtful experiences in your life, we encourage you to look at the process one step at a time. The whole picture is often too much to take in. How do you eat an elephant? One bite at a time. How do you forgive? One person, one act at a time.

Make a list of persons you need to release in the order you feel you need to deal with them.

____

____

____

____

____

Principle #4: Allow Time for the Process to Unfold

This has already been indicated, but it needs to be stated outright. Sometimes, well-meaning people heap guilt upon others by indicating they should be able to forgive as God does. Instantly. That's the way that God forgives, and I am thankful for it. But we are human, we are flesh and blood, and we must live with the frailty of flesh. That isn't an excuse; it's a reality. For humans, forgiveness for the deep hurts that have been perpetrated upon us, often takes time. Again, if you are in the process of moving toward an attitude of forgiveness, that will end in the act of forgiveness, the Father is pleased. Celebrate the process! Don't demand perfection from yourself. He doesn't.

Continue the list of everyone you can think of that you need to forgive.

____

____

____

____

Make a list of the top five things you need to forgive your spouse for.

____

____

____

____

The Forgiveness I Ask from Others (Making Amends)

After the previous discussion, you may be thinking, "I'm not anywhere close to being ready to take this step. I've got too much forgiving I need to do first." Don't be discouraged by that and don't be deterred by it. Both of these processes can happen at the same time. Forgiving others can be a process that takes a good deal of time, just as making amends can be. God knows your heart. He knows if your heart is willing to begin both processes. If you are willing, you can get started in both arenas.

Making amends is more than making an apology. Making amends means that I want to do what I can to make things right. To repair the damage. To make reparations wherever possible. In some situations, a simple apology is all that will be necessary. In some situations, reparations are needed but not possible. In other situations, some actual actions of reparation may be required. When that is the case, an apology by itself is empty and may even be a thinly veiled attempt to escape without fully accepting responsibility.

For instance, there might be some financial reparations that I need to make if I am able. Maybe the reparation is in the form of doing what I can to set a situation right that I have made wrong. If I have gossiped and assassinated someone's character, as a part of my amends to the person I wronged, I should be willing to go back to all the people who heard the gossip and tell them of my wrongdoing. It was a lie. It was wrong. I take responsibility for my wrong and want to do everything in my power to correct it. There are two kinds of amends that can be made and each situation determines which one is appropriate.

Direct Amends

The step says that we make "direct amends to such people wherever possible." This means we go to the person face to face to make amends. Obviously, there are times when this is not physically possible. For instance:

The person is no longer living.

I have no idea where the person is.

The person has no intention of meeting with me.

Are there other situations you can think of?

____

____

____

____

List persons you can think of where direct amends are not possible.

____

____

____

The step goes on to say, "except when to do so would injure them or others."

Sometimes the situation may exist where if I make direct amends, I will cause more damage to the person or to someone else. In that case, direct amends can't be made. I would just create another wrong that I would need to make amends for. Direct amends must never be made when doing so would hurt someone else.

For instance, in the case of sexual infidelity, the spouse of the person with whom I committed the wrong may not even know it happened. My act would certainly be a wrong against the innocent spouse, but to go to them and make amends would not do them any good. I could possibly make direct amends to the person with whom the affair occurred, if the situation allowed it, but that would be the only direct amends I could make without causing further harm.

Another example would be in the case of a destructive attitude you have harbored toward a person. Perhaps they have no knowledge of that attitude. It probably would not be constructive for them for you to go and announce how you have felt about them and then ask their forgiveness for your attitude. You might feel better afterward, but would they? Probably not. You must find another way to make amends.

Sometimes the consequences of direct amends are so enormous that it could cause life-devastating consequences in your own life. In those cases, the consequences must be weighed carefully, and wise counsel sought from a respected individual such as a counselor, pastor, or other person who has been through this process and is able to give guidance.

In those situations where direct amends are neither possible nor wise, there is another kind of amends that can be made.

Indirect Amends

When the situation does not allow for direct amends, the next option is indirect amends. This is where I find a way to make amends that does not directly involve the person I wronged. For instance, if I committed acts of racial violence or treated someone wrongly because of their race and direct amends to that person or persons is not possible, then I might specifically think of ways to treat people of that race in helpful ways as a way of making amends. That would be indirect amends.

If I have wronged someone with whom I can't meet, because it would harm them or because they refuse to meet with me, but I know where they are, I might send a gift or do something positive for them anonymously.

Sometimes indirect amends can be made by writing a letter and expressing my remorse and sorrow over my actions, but then never mailing the letter. This is often helpful when the person has already passed away or I have no knowledge of their whereabouts. The situations are far too diverse and numerous to mention all of them here. The key is to make amends. Do it directly whenever possible and helpful, and when direct amends are not possible, find a way to make indirect amends.

What are some other kinds of indirect amends that you can think of?

____

____

____

Making Your List and Checking It Twice

Now it's time to begin making our list, and like Santa Claus, checking it twice. We want to find out where we have been naughty or nice. Your fourth step is a good place to begin this list. Remember, in the fearless and searching moral inventory of the fourth step, we focused on two things: attitudes and actions. We want to keep it as simple as possible without sacrificing thoroughness. At first, list every person. At the end, you may realize that you are not yet ready to make particular amends. If that is the case, then go on to the ones you are ready to face. In the meantime, pray for the courage, the knowledge, and the will to make those difficult amends in the future. The last two pages of this chapter provide good outlines for the process. First, there is a Marriage Amends form. This focuses on your spouse and the amends you need to make to him/her. Second is the General Amends form for anyone else in your life that you need to make amends to.

What is the most important thing you have learned in this step?

____

____

____

____

What do you intend to do in your marriage this week as a result of this step?

____

____

____

____

TABLE TALK

What is the most important thing about you that relates to this chapter that you are going to share with your spouse this week?

____

____

____

____

MARRIAGE AMENDS

The situation (what happened): ____________________

My attitude: ____________________

My action: ____________________

Direct or indirect amends? ____________________

Why these amends? ____________________

Any reparations I need to make? ____________________

Can I make these amends right now? ____________________

Continue on your own paper . . .

GENERAL AMENDS

The person: ______________________________

The situation (what happened): ______________________________

My attitude: ______________________________

My action: ______________________________

Direct or indirect amends? ______________________________

Why these amends? ______________________________

Any reparations I need to make? ______________________________

Can I make these amends right now? ______________________________

Continue on your own paper . . .

JOURNAL

12

"H"—Heed the Weeds

"We continued to take personal inventory and, when we were wrong, promptly admitted it."

THE PROBLEM OF "H"

The challenge of "H" is complacency! Complacency is a dangerous condition. I know I am there when I become so comfortable that I stop doing the things I need to do. The opposite of complacency is consistency. Consistency is a day-by-day practice of doing the right things because they are the right things to do. Complacency is the enemy of growth and will always lead to backwards movement in any area of life.

My son, Zack, is an accomplished golfer. At this writing, he is playing professional golf. Over the years, Zack has had to make corrections to virtually every part of his golf game in order to keep getting better. With each change, his swing coach would give him drills and exercises to practice. Those drills helped him make the needed changes. For a period of time, he would work on the drill and practice the drill in order to improve his golf swing. As the drill began to have its effect, he would enjoy the benefit of the change. However, invariably over the course of time, he had the tendency to stop doing the drill that brought the change. In his mind, he asked, "Why continue to do the drill? I have made the change. Besides, doing the drill every time I go to the golf course is boring, cumbersome, and takes up valuable practice time." Do you see the fault in that thinking? The things that got him there are the things that would keep him there. The techniques and practice drills that got his swing in such good shape are the disciplines that can keep his swing in good shape if he keeps using them. But, when complacency sets in, the drills stop being used, and then slowly the swing begins to revert. Old habits come back, and some new faulty habits develop. It wasn't until he became a professional that the truth of that principle began to sink in. To succeed at the professional level of golf some daily disciplines are required that are neither fun nor exciting. But, they are necessary.

Another way of expressing this relates to your yard. If you let your yard go for a while, it will eventually fill up with weeds. That's an expression of the second law of thermodynamics that basically says that everything in the universe moves from order to disorder naturally, if left on its own. Nothing moves from disorder to order of its own devices. I once heard it expressed this way. If I place a bunch of marbles on a cookie sheet in a specific order and then begin to shake them, they will forever stay in greater disorder than their original position, no matter how long I shake them. They will never be as ordered as at the beginning, unless some force from the outside imposes order upon them. That would be my hand coming back and putting them in order once again.

That law is demonstrated by as simple a thing as your yard. Recently, my yard had gotten so out of control that I decided to nuke it! That's right. I sprayed weed killer over the entire yard, then tilled up the ground and laid down new sod. That was a drastic measure, but I assure you the situation warranted it. Now I have a freshly sodded yard that's weed-free. I never want my yard to go back into the "weedy" condition it was in. But the sad truth is, if I don't do regular maintenance it won't take all that long before it's right back where it was before. So, I have committed myself to make a daily scan (inventory) of my yard when I drive up the driveway. What will I be looking for? Weeds. One at a time. When I see a weed I intend to root it out right then before it has a chance to grow and spread its weedy seeds. If I can maintain that daily discipline, keeping a weed-free yard is a very real possibility. I never want to have to resort to the "scorched earth" approach again.

The same thing is true of life. Up to this point, if you have genuinely worked this process, you have done some major weeding. You discovered some weeds in your yard. You have learned some skills and acquired some tools for getting the yard cleaned up. Things such as the principle of admitting powerlessness and looking to God who has the power. The process of replacing the lies that have motivated destructive behavior with the truth of God. The grueling task of inventorying your attitudes and actions and taking responsibility for them. Exposing the secrets and going to others to get right. All of these need to be ongoing processes. This step focuses on the need to do continual inventory of attitudes and actions, so that the destructive weeds of those old (and

sometimes new) destructive attitudes and actions can be dealt with as soon as they first appear. I'm like a Weed Warrior. I am on high alert lest any gnarly, nasty, weed pop its ugly little head up in my life. I'm constantly on the lookout for the first sign of it. When I see it I attack it mercilessly and immediately dig it out by the roots. I'm a Weed Warrior on a mission from God!

THE PROCESS OF "H"

Step 4 was a grueling experience. Not something that you want to do every day but something you should have done periodically! So, how do you avoid ever having to do step four again? Keep short accounts. Do smaller inventories on a regular basis. Heed the weeds before you get a yard full of them. Pull them up one at a time on a regular basis, and life is a great deal easier. The following material gives you a couple of yard tools you can use to keep your yard (life and marriage) weed-free if you use them on a daily basis.

The H.O.M.E. Inventory

The H.O.M.E acrostic stands for "Heat Of the Moment Examination." This process is about life change. These steps are tools for life change. If we don't use the tools, then they are wasted and the time spent in acquiring them is wasted. These tools, if you have acquired them, can be carried with you all the time and put to immediate use.

Sometimes the hurtful attitudes and actions we demonstrate toward others happen in the "heat of the moment." You're at work and suddenly have an encounter. You're at home and your spouse says something. In the past, perhaps you had a standard way of reacting in the "heat of the moment" that was destructive and hurtful to yourself, others, and your spouse. The tools you have been acquiring can help you to change those reactions, but you have to use them. Do a H.O.M.E. inventory with the first four steps or principles. It can happen in a few seconds before you respond. For instance, you are at work and someone says something hurtful to you that would normally cause you to go into a funk for the rest of the day. Or maybe your normal reaction would be to bite back and hurt back! You have done this for so long, it's your default position, even though it never brings good results. You just keep doing it over and over.

Perhaps you are home and your spouse says something to you that hurts your feelings or makes you feel rejected or irritated. What would your typical reaction be? Probably not something constructive. In that instant, you could do a H.O.M.E. inventory in your mind and change a *reaction* into a *response*.

A Admit Powerlessness. I am powerless over this person, and if I react my life (day) is going to become unmanageable. I can't change them and I can't control them, and it is foolish for me to try.

B Believe the Truth. I don't have to strike back. I don't have to defend. The truth is, "This isn't really about me; it's about them."

C Confess Christ. Okay, Jesus, you have to intervene here. I confess you as Lord of this situation. I turn my will over to you right now to do and say what you want me to do and say, not what I want!

D Discover Responsibility. What is my responsibility in this situation? Have I done something to provoke him/her? Was I insensitive? Did I fail to do what I should have done and are they only reacting to my irresponsibility? Is there anything I need to own?

It may sound as if that would take a great deal of time, but it will take only a few seconds. By the time I have focused my mind on that process and away from reacting, I can respond instead. I can be controlled by Christ rather than by the situation or person. When I act under His control, the result is always going to be better. The following graphic illustrates this process.

As long as I am directed by my feelings, I will continue to react to things that happen during my day. Things people say and do will cause me to react with predictable feelings, thoughts, and actions. They are predictable because I have done them over and over for so long. My life is stuck in the circle of insanity going around and around. Reactions are always negative. My life is out of control and unmanageable. In fact, I become like the ball in a pinball machine. Bouncing around from one reaction to another. Something has to happen to break the circle of insanity. I have to do something different. I need a breakpoint. That can come when I choose, as an act of the will, to break the circle by stopping before I react and using the tools of A.B.C. and D. That creates a breakpoint in the circle and allows me to enter into another circle, which is the circle of sanity. I can then respond based upon fact not feelings. Responses are healthy and helpful. Reactions are harmful and hurtful.

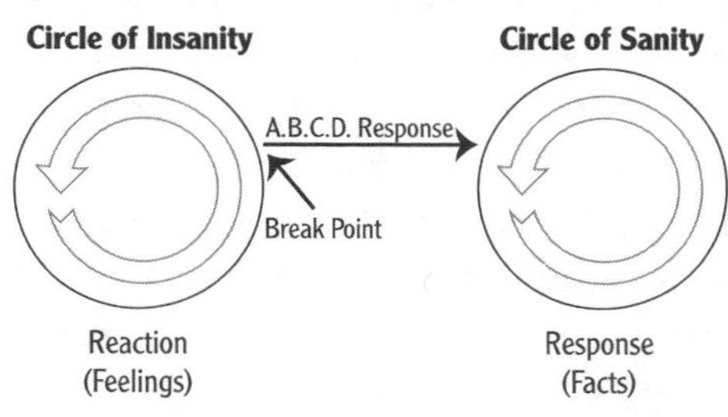

I may feel like reacting, but I can choose to respond if I choose to act upon facts. I am powerless, and if I try to control this person or situation my moment, day, life, is going to become unmanageable. God is able, so I turn my will over to Him and focus on my responsibility in the situation. I have just done A.B.C.D. and broken the circle of insanity.

Remember the discussion about talking to yourself back in "F": Focus on Faith? This is the practical application of how to talk to yourself. In the heat of the moment, don't listen to yourself. Talk to yourself! Talk to yourself! Talk to yourself!

Discovery: When I change my reactions to responses, it will often change the way others act toward me.

It's like a little boy throwing a baseball against a wall. As long as the wall keeps bouncing the ball back, he will keep throwing at the wall. However, if for some reason the ball stops coming back to him, he'll soon stop throwing it. It's no fun to throw at an object that gives no bounceback. When we change our reactions to responses, we stop giving the bounceback and all the fun is taken away for the other person. Get it?

List some scenarios where you could practice a H.O.M.E. inventory with your spouse:

____

____

____

____

In what ways would practicing the H.O.M.E. inventory change you?

____

____

____

____

How might it impact your relationship with your spouse and others?

1. Spouse ____________________________________

2. Children __________________________________

3. Friends ____

4. Work ____

The E.D. Inventory

Who's Ed? In this case, Ed isn't a person, or a talking horse, but a process. It's the "End of Day" inventory. If we were perfect with the H.O.M.E. inventory we wouldn't need the E.D. inventory. But the truth is, we aren't. Sometimes, in the heat of the moment, we don't get it just right, so that is when we need the E.D. inventory.

One Sunday morning in the service in our church, I was teaching on an important but controversial subject. It's a subject that fires me up every time I think about it, because it is perpetrated upon so many well-meaning Christians and is used to lead many away from the simple truth of the Scriptures. (I can feel myself getting fired up right now!) Anyway, after the second service, a man I met nearly thirty years ago came up to discuss it with me. Actually, he wanted to express some disagreement with me about the topic. I immediately powered up on him and blew him away.

Having confessed that, now it's important to mention a couple of things. These things don't excuse my behavior. There was no excuse for that. But they do give some explanation.

First, right after the second service on Sunday morning is not the best time to approach me to discuss a question like that. I am worn out, spent, and tired of talking. Second, I had a deadline to meet. I needed to be in Dallas within forty-five minutes of the close of the second service, and I knew I was going to be stretched to get there even if I got away immediately. So his need to discuss the issue immediately stressed me and made me impatient, and I reacted unkindly and shut him down.

As I was driving to Dallas I began to think about the encounter and immediately admitted to myself that I had been wrong. I spent the afternoon in Dallas focusing on what I had to be there for and didn't have much time to think about it again until that night back at home. That was when I did an E.D. inventory. That was all I had left because, obviously, I hadn't done a H.O.M.E. inventory and, consequently, had reacted in a way I shouldn't have.

In my E.D. inventory, I admitted my wrong to myself and to God. I accepted my responsibility for what had happened. He had done nothing wrong. He had no knowledge of my time schedule. He wanted to discuss something that was important to him and right then seemed a fine time to get it done. The responsibility was all mine.

I committed myself right then that the next day I would do everything in my power to make it right. The next morning, to my chagrin, I discovered that I had neither a phone number for him nor any kind of address. He was not a member of the church. However, I did find an email address for his wife at her workplace. I immediately wrote an email to him expressing my sorrow about the way I had behaved. I asked for his forgiveness for the way I had treated him. Then I sent it to his wife, with an introduction asking her to be sure that he got it. Then I copied it to my senior associate on the church staff. I felt I needed to confess what I had done to another person.

Here is the truth. Because I had failed to do a H.O.M.E. inventory and practice the tools of A, B, C, and D, then in my E.D. inventory I had to go on and practice E, F, and G! I had to expose the secret. I confessed to myself, God and not one other person but two! His wife and my associate. Then I had to "Focus on Faith," and that meant to do what God told me to do. If I want God to remove this defect of character, that means I have to do what He tells me to do in His Word. Repent and seek forgiveness. Then, I had to "Go and Get Right" by making amends.

I could have saved myself the time of having to practice E, F, and G in my E.D. inventory if I had just practiced A, B, C, and D in a H.O.M.E. inventory! Are you confused? I hope not. The next time I am in one of those heat-of-the-moment situations I hope I remember to do a H.O.M.E. inventory. But if I fail again, which I probably will, at least I have the E.D. inventory. (An E.D. Inventory Worksheet is provided at the end of this chapter.) With these two types of inventories, I'm "Heeding the Weeds." Fighting the battle. Doing the work of the Weed Warrior.

What is the most important thing you have learned from this step?

____

____

____

____

What do you intend to do in your marriage this week as a result of this step?

____

____

____

____

____

TABLE TALK

What is the most important thing about you that relates to this chapter that you are going to share with your spouse this week?

____

____

____

____

E.D. INVENTORY WORKSHEET

Assets of the Day

Healthy emotions and attitudes I demonstrated today.

____

____

____

____

Positive actions I demonstrated today.

____

____

____

____

Liabilities of the Day

Negative emotions and attitudes I demonstrated today.

____

____

____

____

Negative actions I demonstrated today.

____

____

H.O.M.E. inventories I did today.

Amends I need to make to my spouse or others from today's attitudes and actions.

JOURNAL

13

"I"—Increase God Contact

"We sought through prayer and meditation to improve our conscious contact with God, praying only for knowledge of His will for us and the power to carry that out."

THE PROBLEM OF "I"

The problem of "I" is that a void has been created through the practice of A through H that needs to be filled. If you are practicing those principles each day, some things are beginning to change. You have begun removing some things from your life. Hopefully, you are no longer as filled with yourself if you have "Admitted Powerlessness" and continue to do so every day. You have identified some lies that were driving your life in B. You have made the decision to vacate the driver's seat of your life in C. You have discovered your responsibility and exposed the secrets in steps D and E. You get the idea. Your life has been filled with attitudes and actions that were destructive and you have been busy doing some house cleaning. Many of the things that hindered an intimate relationship with God are in the process of being removed and that has created a void. In step "I" we focus on filling that void with some habits that can help promote an increasingly intimate relationship with the One who has desired that intimacy with you from the beginning.

There are a couple of scriptural images that will help you understand what "I" is all about. In Romans 12:2, we are encouraged to stop being "conformed to this world" and to be "transformed by the renewing of…[our] mind." That's what steps A through H have been focusing on. Then the verse goes on and expresses the reason we need to be transformed by the renewing of our minds. So that we may "prove what the will of God is, that which is good and acceptable and perfect." In "I," we now express our desire to know His will, to be guided by His will, and to be empowered to do His will as we walk with Him!

In Romans 7, Paul expresses his distress about the struggle between the Spirit and the flesh in his own life. He says the things he wants to do he doesn't do and the things he doesn't want to do he finds himself doing. We can all relate to that. We all fight that fight. We are involved in spiritual war between the flesh and the Spirit. Someone once said, "If you have two dogs in a fight, which one is going to win?" The answer, "The one you feed the most." The one you feed the most will be the strongest.

"I" is about feeding the right dog. We recognize that if we stop practicing A through H, then the "bad dog" is going to get strong again. We want to starve that dog by continuing to practice those principles. At the same time we want to feed the "good dog"—the "dog of the Spirit." Steps A through H are about starving the mongrel dog of the flesh and "I" is about feeding the pedigree dog of the Spirit. It's as simple as that.

In what specific ways have you been starving the "flesh dog" in this process?

____

____

____

____

THE PROCESS OF "I"

In step "I," we are talking about the Christian disciplines as tools for "Increasing God" contact. Historically, the disciplines refer to prayer, fasting, worship, and reading, studying, and memorizing Scripture along with several other disciplines. They're all important for any believer who desires to move deeper into intimacy with the Father. However, I am going to make a statement I know will be controversial for some. The Christian disciplines are not by themselves the way to increased contact with God.

I remember a very painful time in my life when I was practicing the Christian disciplines more than I ever had before. But during that time, I continued to spiral down into a darkness that at times made me wonder if I would survive. I was up in the wee hours of the morning on my face before God praying. I memorized entire books of the Bible, not just verses. In fact, during that I time I memorized Philippians, Ephesians, and James, word for word! I couldn't understand why God wasn't responding to my cries and my discipline. It wasn't until years later that I began to understand the problem. The disciplines themselves are just religious activity with no power, no effect, and virtually no value, unless the emotional blocks that keep them from having their effect are recognized, dealt with, and removed.

It's a little like the Old Testament Hebrew people. They had the sacrificial system that God had given them. He instructed them specifically what sacrifices to bring, how to bring them, and when to bring them. This was a major discipline they were to practice before Him. However, repeatedly they fell into disobedience and even idolatry. They would chase after the false gods of the nations around them and intermarry with them, even though God had specifically forbidden that practice. And, during that time, they would continue to practice the discipline of sacrifice. They kept bringing their sacrifices to God. His response was to inform them that what He really desired was obedience, not sacrifice. Their sacrifices and discipline, offered during their disobedience, made Him sick to His stomach.

It makes very little sense for us to think that our disciplines of prayer, worship, Bible study, and fasting are going to have any effect while we are operating in our own pride, living double lives by keeping secrets, or harboring unforgiveness and an unwillingness to own responsibility for our bad choices. If we are unwilling to go to those we have wronged and seek to make it right with them, how can the Christian disciplines have any power? What if we are trying to live *in* God's promises but are unwilling to live *by* God's premises? Does it make any sense that our practice of the disciplines would have any value at all? While our lives are in that condition, would the practice of the Christian disciplines have the same effect on the Father that the Hebrew people's sacrifices had while they were chasing after other gods? Don't they make Him sick as well? Aren't they just empty religious ritual? I think so.

Recently, my Saturday morning men's group was working through these principles. We meet in a large group and then break off into small groups. We were dealing with this step that morning and I was explaining the importance of the first ten steps for removing the barriers so the Christian disciplines could have their benefit. Afterwards one of the men came to me to tell his testimony. He had been raised up as a Christian adult under the Navigators, a wonderful Christian organization that emphasizes the discipline of the Word—study, memorization, and meditation upon it. He told me that he had practiced the disciplines very faithfully for years. Then in 2000 his marriage nearly fell apart. He identified the issues that precipitated that fracture as control and anger. He said even in that time he never stopped the disciplines. But he told me that when he got into this process and began to discover the source of his control and anger things began to change. He said, "Not only did things begin to change in me but my marriage began to change." "Now," he said, "I practice the Christian disciplines, but with a completely different spirit. Now they have real meaning in my life." I asked him to share that testimony with his men's group that morning and asked if I could share that testimony here. He has lived out this truth.

That's why this step is almost at the end of the process! We have been discovering principles and gaining tools by which we can deal with the issues that render the disciplines powerless! We have been learning how to starve the flesh dog so that now we can feed the Spirit dog. All of the spiritual disciplines will not be dealt with here. Christians should seek them out as they continue to mature. However, there are three disciplines I want to mention and develop in order to help you get started: the Word, prayer, and confession.

The Discipline of the Word

I remember many years ago in college, being exposed to the "hand" illustration that originated with the Navigators. The hand has five fingers, and each finger represents an increasingly important activity that relates to the Word of God, the Bible. As each finger is added, our grip on the Word and its grip on us grows stronger. I have changed it a little, but the overall idea is the same.

Of course, the weakest grip is to just read the Word. That really isn't any grip at all! That's just one finger. But when I add the study of the Word it gets stronger. Now I have a two-finger grip. Then come memorization, meditation, and application. When I have all five fingers working, then I have a strong grip on the Word, and it has its impact in my life. I have never forgotten this illustration, and it has guided me through the years. The truth is, many stop with reading the Word. A much smaller percentage of Christians study Scripture. After that, it falls off to a very small percentage who memorize, meditate upon, and seek to apply its principles in every situation.

Here is a question. What good is it to study something that you can't recall? Suppose I am a student in a math class and I study how to multiply. Is there value in that? Yes, but not much! We did much more than just study multiplication, didn't we? We memorized the multiplication tables! Why? So we would have not only an understanding of the principles of multiplication but also would be able to carry them with us to use in daily life. If I am the student who has only studied multiplication but hasn't memorized the tables, then that study isn't much practical good for me, is it?

If I walk into a store with a quarter in my pocket and I want three suckers that are ten cents apiece, and I haven't memorized that 3x10 is thirty, I will have no way of knowing if I have enough money or not. My study of multiplication is useless because I didn't carry the information with me through memorization. The same is true of God's Word. It's of no practical value to me until I internalize it enough to carry it with me!

There are three benefits that the believer can derive from the Word when he/she has a five-finger grip on it.

Faith

> *Faith comes from hearing and hearing by the word of Christ. (Romans 10:17)*

If, as has already been discovered in a previous chapter, faith is simply taking God at His Word, then I can't exercise faith without knowledge of what God has said! If I don't have a firm grasp of what God has said, how can I believe Him? So, an increased knowledge or grasp upon the Word gives me greater opportunity to exercise faith and take God at His Word. It doesn't guarantee it, but it provides opportunity for it.

Guidance

> *Your word is a lamp to my feet and a light to my path. (Psalm 119:105)*

In essence, the psalmist is saying God's Word is like a flashlight that lights my way in the darkness. If you have ever been out of doors much, you know that when you get away from city lights, it can really get dark. When the skies are overcast and the moon is not out, it can be pitch black. When it's like that, you need a flashlight to light the way so you don't stumble over things and even fall into a crevice or off a cliff. The flashlight you have at home in the garage doesn't do you much good. You need it in your hand right then.

The Word is like that flashlight. When it's dark you need its guidance. The Bible at home on the coffee table isn't going to do you any good. You need the Bible in your mind and heart so that wherever you go and whatever you do, you can access it, shine it in the darkness you are facing, and walk in its light. If you haven't committed it to memory, how can it light your way in the darkness?

Transformation

> *And do not be conformed to this world, but be transformed by the renewing of your mind. (Romans 12:2a)*

As we have already studied, change begins with the mind. Beliefs. This passage reminds us that we are transformed by the "renewing" of our mind. Change happens when we replace the lies of the world, flesh, and Enemy with the truth of God. What is the truth of God? His Word.

> *"Sanctify them in the truth; Your word is truth." (John 17:17)*

Once again, internalizing the Word through memorization so that you can meditate upon the Word during the day is part of the process of replacing destructive lies of the Enemy with the truth of God.

What level of internalization of the Scriptures has been your practice up to now?

____

____

Would you commit yourself to memorizing and meditating on one verse of Scripture per week as a part of this step of "I"—Increasing God Contact?

____

____

____

____

If you said "Yes," begin in the Gospel of John. Beginning with chapter 1, pick a key verse out of that chapter and memorize and meditate upon it this week. Do that each week with a new chapter.

What discipline do you need to begin in order to be "in the Word" (e.g., join a Bible class at church, set a daily study time, etc.)?

____

____

____

____

The Discipline of Prayer

Prayer is perhaps one of the most misunderstood and misapplied disciplines of the Christian life. Much of what is taught and practiced about prayer doesn't contribute to our practice of it but discourages most of us away from it! That's a sad condition to be in. Prayer is not a tool by which we wrest from the hand of a stingy God the things we want and need in life—presenting our laundry list of needs and wants to God so He can fill our basket. I want to mention three things that true prayer is which will encourage you to enter into the process with joy and real meaning.

Prayer Is Conversation

Prayer isn't a lecture from our side or God's side. A lecture is one-way communication. One person talks and everyone else listens. A conversation is communication where two people talk and listen. Prayer is a process by which we speak to God and we listen to Him. We expect Him to speak to us. How does He speak? Obviously, He speaks to us through His Word. But He also speaks to us through His indwelling Spirit. This will often come in those moments of sudden clarity about an issue we have been speaking to God about. It will sometimes come through a gentle impression the Spirit gives to direct us in something we have been seeking God's guidance about. We speak to God, but we must then listen and wait for Him to speak to us in return. He will sometimes speak through an impression of the Holy Spirit within. He may speak through another person of wise counsel we trust and respect. He can even speak to us through circumstances. There are many ways God may speak to us, but one thing is always true. His Word is the ultimate standard of truth.

Anything we sense God is telling us must always be measured against His revealed Word. He will never say something through an impression of the Spirit or any other means that contradicts His written Word. Everything must always be evaluated and measured against His Word. If it's not in line with His Word, then it's not from Him. He will not contradict His Word.

Prayer is conversation. Times of speaking to God and times of silence in order to listen for His voice.

What are some other ways that God might speak to you?

____

____

____

____

What is the ultimate standard by which everything is measured?

____

____

____

____

Prayer Is Communion

Conversation is how people get to know one another. When a young man and woman first begin dating it's talk, talk, talk. Why? Two people are getting to know one another! Often, the young woman's complaint is that after the marriage began the conversation stopped! That's often a sad, but true, scenario. When couples stop talking, they begin drifting apart. Conversation is a way by which we commune with one another and with God. Prayer is communion between the child of God and the heavenly Father.

Prayer Is Continual

Pray without ceasing. (1 Thessalonians 5:17)

In other words, real prayer is a continual process. Prayer is like dialing a number on the telephone and when the person answers on the other end you leave the connection open all day long. The phone line is always open and at any moment the two can speak to each other.

My children are both grown now, but I still have an agreement with them that I made when they were little. Whenever they call me, I will take their call. No matter what I am doing, I take their call. Anytime, night or day, when I look at the caller ID and it tells me it is one of my children, I stop what I am doing and take the call. Why? As their father, I want them to know that in whatever circumstances they might find themselves, if they need or want to talk to me, nothing else will ever be more important to me. They don't have to make an appointment or get in line to talk to me. I take the call. So does our heavenly Father. No appointment necessary. He takes the call.

I am convinced that many Christians have concentrated so much on establishing a habitual prayer time that they have lost the *process* of prayer. We have placed a great deal of emphasis on the need to set aside a portion of the day for prayer—usually, it's stressed that morning is the best time to meet with God. While I also believe that it's a good and important thing to do, the purpose of a scheduled prayer time should be to *begin the process of prayer for the day*. To "open the phone line" (if you will) for the day. If your prayer time doesn't begin the *process* of prayer, it will eventually become just another ritual.

Far too often, Christians make a "contract" to meet with God at a set place and time for prayer, but then miss the power of continual prayer. As you learn to have conversation with God and commune with Him through prayer, remember that He desires to have the lines open to you all day, every day, in any circumstance. In those moments when you face challenges, temptations, or struggles, know that the line is open and the Father is able and eager to hear your cry for help, understanding, strength, or whatever you need at the time. You could call this "practicing the presence of God" all through the day. If there is no need that you are bringing to Him, then bring praise to Him. Give Him thanks for His blessings. Have conversation and communion continually as you move through your day.

How much of your praying consists of speaking and how much of listening?

____

____

____

____

When you pray, what is typically your main purpose? Communion with God or to carry out your "contract" with God?

____

____

____

____

How can you practice the concept of continual prayer in your daily life?

____

____

____

____

The Discipline of Confession

In step "E"—Expose the Secrets, we dealt with confession. Confession in the original language of the New Testament means to "speak the same as." It has the idea of "coming into agreement." As we said then, when we confess our sin to God, we aren't telling Him anything He doesn't know. We are coming into agreement with what He already knows is true. Confession is the way by which we keep short accounts.

We know that when we have wronged someone in a human relationship, we have to admit it, confess it, and accept responsibility for our wrongful action. The longer it takes us to come to that place, the more damage is done in the relationship and the more difficult it becomes for us to admit our mistake. It's always better for the relationship if we confess our fault quickly. Not only that, but it's easier to do it quickly than it is after we have denied it and avoided it for a long period of time.

We must also keep short accounts with God. Why? Because unconfessed sin has the same damaging effect on our ability to have an intimate relationship with God as it has in human relationships. If we are genuinely His through faith in Christ, He never rejects us as His children, but our unwillingness to confess our sin to Him definitely causes a block in our ability to experience intimacy in the relationship. This is true because of the effect unconfessed sin has on the Holy Spirit who dwells within all true believers.

The importance of the Holy Spirit's ministry in the life of the believer cannot be overstated. Just a few things that the Holy Spirit does are:

1. Guides into truth—John 16:13

2. Empowers—Acts 1:8

3. Helps, comforts, encourages—John 14:16-17; Acts 9:31

4. Convicts—John 16:8

5. Intercedes—Romans 8:27

6. Assures and secures—Romans 8:16; Ephesians 1:13-14

All of these are incredibly important in the Christian life! As you can tell from this short list, growth and intimacy with the Father is dependent upon the Holy Spirit having the freedom to perform His ministry in the life of the Christian. Confession is so important to intimacy with God because of the wreckage that unconfessed sin brings upon the Holy Spirit's ability to perform His ministry. The Bible indicates two very important effects that unconfessed sin has upon the Holy Spirit.

Sin Grieves the Holy Spirit

Throughout the New Testament, the Holy Spirit is revealed as a *person,* not an *it. Things* don't experience grief. Only beings can do that.

> *Do not grieve the Holy Spirit of God, by whom you were sealed for the day of redemption. (Ephesians 4:30)*

The context of that statement is within a discussion of things that believers are to avoid such as bitterness, wrath, slander, and the list goes on. Why? Because these things wound the Holy Spirit. They cause the Holy Spirit in the believer grief and pain.

Sin Quenches the Holy Spirit

Do not quench the Spirit. (1 Thessalonians 5:19)

This time, the context is within a discussion of things that the believer is to do, such as pray without ceasing in addition to avoiding behavior such as repaying evil for evil. Paul goes on to say in verses 21–22, to "Hold fast to that which is good; abstain from every form of evil." Why? Because it quenches the Holy Spirit!

Often in the Bible, one of the symbols used for the Holy Spirit is fire. What does water do to a fire? It puts it out! It quenches it! When a fire is quenched, it can't give warmth, it can't be used to cook, it can't purify.

When the Holy Spirit in the believer is grieved and quenched because of unconfessed sin, He can't do His work in the believer's life. All of the things He does are important, but for this discussion of "increasing our conscious contact with God," His witness in our hearts that we are children of God is especially important. The Holy Spirit is the means by which we have communion with God, who is Spirit. If the Holy Spirit is hindered in me because of sin I have not acknowledged, owned, and confessed, then He cannot do His work of communion with the Father.

So, it is very important that we keep short accounts with God. When we have acted in our own self-will rather than in obedience to Him, that is called sin. God knows it is sin, and when His Spirit convicts me of sin there is only one solution. Turn from it and confess it to Him for what it is. Sin. That keeps the fire of the Spirit burning bright in the believer's life so that the Spirit isn't grieved or quenched. He has full, unhindered freedom to do His ministry in our lives and increase our sense of intimacy with the heavenly Father.

The H.O.M.E. and E.D. inventories are both tools that we can use to keep short accounts with the heavenly Father and keep the fires burning. When we discover wrong attitudes and actions through these inventories, then it's time to take it to the Father in confession.

What is the most important thing you have learned in this step?

____

____

What do you intend to do this week as a result of this step?

____

____

TABLE TALK

What is the most important thing about you that relates to this chapter that you are going to share with your spouse this week?

JOURNAL

14

"J"—Just Do It!

"Having had a spiritual awakening as the result of these Steps, we tried to carry this message to others, and to practice these principles in all our affairs."

THE PROBLEM OF "J"

This step assumes that you have worked through the previous steps and have, to some extent, begun to experience true life change. It's my conviction that you cannot have genuinely understood and begun practicing these principles without experiencing some change. If you have begun to experience change, then you are in a spiritual awakening! Therefore, the first challenge this step presents is for us to take an honest assessment to evaluate that change and spiritual awakening.

What has God shown you about Himself, yourself, and others in this process?

1. About God ____

2. About Yourself ______________________________________

3. About Your Spouse ___________________________________

Take a moment to evaluate areas where you have begun to see change. Remember, any change at all is change! Attitudes, actions, relationships . . .

1. ____

2. ____

3. ____

The second problem this step presents is that it challenges us to be consistent. Life change is a lifelong process. It isn't something that is accomplished in a number of weeks in a freedom group. This process is for getting to the truth, acquiring new tools, and learning along with others how to use those tools in life. Life change should last a lifetime as you uncover more of the truth and become more skilled at using the tools that you have now acquired. It's easy to go up like a rocket and come down like a rock. This step challenges us to accept the fact that we have not finished the race. We have just come out of the starting block and the track now stretches before us.

So, assuming that your answer is that you have experienced, and are experiencing, a spiritual awakening, the question is, "What do I do now?" Well, just do it! Just do what? Three things.

THE PROCESS OF "J"

Practice, Practice, Practice

One time, I asked my dear friend, Chuck, how he had become an alcoholic. His response (with a grin on his face) was, "Practice, practice, practice." Chuck has now been sober twenty years. When someone asks him how he stays sober, he says (with a grin on his face), "Practice, practice, practice." Either way, it's all about practice. He became good at his alcoholism through practice. He has become good at sobriety through practice.

Chuck has always understood that the things he had to do to get sober are the things he has to continue to do to stay sober. That's true of any change. The things you had to do in order to make the change are the things you have to do to maintain the change. Most of us spent years "practicing" our destructive attitudes and actions. Now we need to spend years practicing new attitudes and actions.

These principles don't just apply in a few areas of our lives, either. They apply to every attitude, every action, every relationship, and every situation! In other words, we want to practice them in "all our affairs," as the step says. We don't want to compartmentalize life. We want every area of life to be changed by the practice of these principles.

This is so important because if we aren't practicing these principles, then we can't do the other things this step is about. Practice gives me the moral ground to do the other things I need to do. This is the proverbial "where the rubber meets the road" step. This is where the sheep are separated from the goats, the men from the boys, the women from the girls, the snakes from the lizards...you get the idea. So, what is it that we are to practice? Let's review.

1. A: Admit Powerlessness—At any moment that I step out of my powerlessness, I step into the flesh and into true weakness. Daily, moment by moment I have to "speak to myself" about this truth.
2. B: Believe the Truth—The lies of the Enemy and the world will constantly bombard me for the rest of my life here on earth. I am weak, He is strong. The Enemy is a liar; Jesus is the Truth. Therefore, I have to "come to believe" every day—always on my guard against the lies that want to creep in and deceive me and always seeking the truth about God, self, and others.
3. C: Commit to Christ—This doesn't mean I receive Christ as my Savior over and over again each day. No, that has to happen only once for me to become His child by faith. But every day I have to submit to His lordship. That means I have to submit my will each day. Submit, each day, the care of my life to Him.
4. D: Discover Responsibility—In every situation, relationship, and conflict, the first thing I must do is examine my heart to see if there is something that I need to own.
5. E: Expose the Secrets—Secrets kill. Secrets make me sick, so I must keep my hospital gown open in the back. Fight against "image management" and covering up what is truly going on inside.
6. F: Focus on Faith—What I want to do is live in the promise, so I have to daily live by the premise. Obey God and His Word and trust Him to do what He has promised in my life.
7. G: Go Get Right—When I am wrong, I want to keep short accounts. Don't let them build up into a giant heap, but deal with them one at a time as they arise.
8. H: Heed the Weeds—Daily inventory is a vital part of the process. I must do "heat of the moment" H.O.M.E. inventories (A, B, C, D) all day long. At the end of the day, I do an E.D. inventory to identify anytime when I didn't do the H.O.M.E. and therefore reacted badly. Then I must do E, F, and G as soon as possible.
9. I: Increase God Contact—Practice the disciplines that will continue to move me toward deeper and deeper intimacy with my heavenly Father.
10. J: Just Do It—Consistently apply the principles and use the tools provided in these steps throughout my life. Then carry this message to others.

The value of these principles isn't found in knowing them but in doing them.

These principles are not just for study, but practice! This process is about life change. Jesus communicated it very clearly.

> *"Therefore everyone who hears these words of Mine and acts on them, may be compared to a wise man who built his house on the rock. And the rain fell, and the floods came, and the winds blew and slammed against that house; and yet it did not fall, for it had been founded on the rock." (Matthew 7:24–25)*

Many of us have built our lives upon a very shaky foundation. The foundation of self-will, rather than His will. The foundation of my way, rather than His way. It's time to rebuild upon the solid rock of practice, practice, practice!

> *But prove yourselves doers of the word, and not merely hearers who delude themselves. For if anyone is a hearer of the word and not a doer, he is like a man who looks at his natural face in a mirror; for once he has looked at himself and gone away, he has immediately forgotten what kind of person he was. But one who looks intently at the perfect law, the law of liberty, and abides by it, not having become a forgetful hearer but an effectual doer, this man will be blessed in what he does. (James 1:22–25)*

Which of these principles has been the easiest for you to practice daily? ____________

____

Why? ____

Which has been the most difficult? Why? ____________________________

____

What do you need to do in order to become more consistent in your weaker areas?

____

Preach, Preach, Preach

Notice that practice comes before preaching. If it doesn't, then preaching is empty, isn't it? People look at our lives before they hear what we say. Mahatma Gandhi once said, "I would have become a Christian if it hadn't been for the Christians I knew." That's the tragedy of preaching without practice. The Bible calls that hypocrisy, and people sniff it out pretty quickly!

While we endeavor to practice, practice, practice, the next thing we are to do is preach, preach, preach. I know that strikes a negative chord in a lot of people's minds right now. Why? Because we have turned that word into a kind of negative, haven't we? We say to someone, "Don't preach to me!" But, if you understand what it means, it isn't negative at all. In the original language of the New Testament, the word "preach" meant to announce something. It was used to describe the action of a herald who went through the streets announcing the latest news. In essence, the word "preach" simply means to tell what you know. If you know something good, then tell it. That's preaching!

> *"What I tell you in the darkness, speak in the light; and what you hear whispered in your ear, proclaim upon the housetops." (Matthew 10:27)*

What Do I Preach?

Since you have come this far in the process, there are some things you know. In other words, you have discovered some things that you are seeking to practice in your life daily. These are things that are bringing you *help, hope,* and *healing*. This step simply says, "Be willing to tell that!" Be willing to tell others about your *help, hope,* and *healing*.

What are some things that you know from this process that you can preach?

____

____

____

____

What you just wrote down is a four-point sermon! You're ready to preach. You have a text, you have an outline, and you have experience! Preach it! You don't have to go to seminary or Bible school. You are in the best Bible school on the planet; you've been to the school of life change. You are practicing the principles. Life change—preach it!

How Do I Preach?

You just tell the things that you know. Tell your story of *help, hope,* and *healing*. Tell the things that you know as you go through the normal course of life and encounter people. You don't have to convince them, control them, chide them, or convert them. You just have to tell them. What they do with the news is their responsibility. Delivering the news is your responsibility. The results are up to God.

We aren't talking about cramming something down someone's throat. That never has worked, although many have tried it. Anything I cram down someone's throat they will just throw up as soon as I let them up. The only thing people keep down, and digest, and find nourishment for their soul from is what they swallow on their own.

I love the story in John 9, where Jesus healed a man who had been blind from birth. The healing caused the Pharisees a great deal of anxiety, so they cross-examined the man not once but two times, trying to discredit the miracle of Jesus. They argued with him about the character of Jesus, calling Him a sinner because He had done this on the Sabbath. They grilled him about the identity of Jesus. Then, they went to the man's parents and questioned them. When they came back to the man a second time, the simplicity and power of his response said it all.

> *He then answered, "Whether He is a sinner, I do not know; one thing I do know, that though I was blind, now I see." (John 9:25)*

That's what he knew and that's what he preached. I was blind and now I see. The evidence was there. They couldn't refute it no matter how hard they tried. Here was a man born blind who now could see. His sermon was simple but powerful. This is what I know.

Where Do I Preach?

Simple answer. Wherever you are and whatever you are doing. There is never a time and never a place where truth isn't appropriate. That is, truth that is delivered in love, in humility, without arrogance.

> *Preach the word; be ready in season and out of season. (2 Timothy 4:2)*

There is never a time or place when I am not to be ready to preach. I carry my sermon with me everywhere I go. It's my story of *help*, *hope*, and *healing*. I don't need notes, I don't need to study. I am studying every day of my life as I practice these principles. My preparation is life change, and it's with me everywhere I go.

> *And Jesus came up and spoke to them, saying, "All authority has been given to Me in heaven and on earth. Go therefore and make disciples of all the nations . . ." (Matthew 28:18–19a)*

Jesus charged every Christian to be a disciple maker. He said, "Go and make disciples . . . ." In the original language the word "go" is in a verb tense that means continuous action. It could literally be translated "Go, and as you are going. . . ." I love that Jesus made disciple-making a natural process of everyday living. I'm to be a disciple maker as I'm going. Go to work, and as you are working. . . . Go to play and as you are playing . . . . Go to the mall and as you are shopping . . . . It's simply to become a natural part of life. I am to be ready. There is never a closed season on telling my story of *help, hope,* and *healing* in Jesus Christ. The season is open 24/7/365! Anywhere life presents the opportunity, you can speak of your story without being obnoxious or pushy or rude. In the natural course of life, as situations arise where it is appropriate, tell your story naturally as it applies to the situation.

If you have experienced some *help, hope,* and *healing* in your marriage over these weeks of this freedom group, how can you keep that to yourself? How many other couples out there need to hear your story? Will you tell it?

Think of some situations where you can preach.

____

____

____

____

> *"But you will receive power when the Holy Spirit has come upon you; and you shall be My witnesses both in Jerusalem, and in all Judea and Samaria, and even to the remotest part of the earth." (Acts 1:8)*

Jesus spoke these words after His resurrection, just before He ascended to the heavens. His words here are a restatement of His great commission to His followers. He said it a little differently this time.

Jesus was giving each of us a strategic plan for carrying this message of life change. It's a ripple effect, like dropping a stone in water and then the concentric circles spread from the center outward. They were in Jerusalem at the time. That's where they lived. That's where they were to begin, and it's where they did begin. Then the message spread to the surrounding region of Judea, then into Samaria, and eventually to the far corners of the earth.

You might ask yourself, "Where do I start?" Begin in your Jerusalem. With those that are closest to you. Your family. That's your Jerusalem. Then Judea—friends and associates. Then Samaria. Samaria represented people that, as Jews, the disciples had been taught to have no contact with. The Samaritans were the result of intermarrying between Jews and Gentiles, and they were to be avoided at all costs. That no longer applied in Christ. He said tell the Samaritans because the message is for them as well. Then to the remotest parts of the earth. Wherever you are, wherever you can, by whatever means you have, carry the message of *help, hope,* and *healing* in Christ.

Who is in your Jerusalem? ____

____

Your Judea? ____

____

Your Samaria? ____

____

How Will They Ever Know If Someone Doesn't Tell Them?

You say, "Well, I will just let my life be my witness." Without doubt, our lives are certainly important. We have already established that. When people look at my life, they can see the changes that are happening in me. But how will they know the source of those changes if I don't tell them? Can they discern just by observation what the ultimate source of the *help, hope,* and *healing* is? No, I have to tell them. So, we preach first with our lives and then with our lips. Lives and lips. Both are important and are important in that order. The Scripture lays this principle out clearly and beautifully.

> *For "whoever will call upon the name of the Lord will be saved." How then will they call on Him in whom they have not believed? How will they believe in Him whom they have not heard? And how will they hear without a preacher? How will they preach unless they are sent? Just as it is written, "How beautiful are the feet of those who bring good news of good things!" (Romans 10:13–15)*

Feet aren't normally something we speak of as being beautiful. But even the most calloused, gnarly, and ugly feet become beautiful when they are used to deliver the good news. You want to have beautiful feet in God's eyes? Use them to carry the message. Use them to take you places where people need to hear how you found what they are seeing in your life.

We are all called to be preachers, and we have all been sent by Jesus. Now we just have to preach, preach, preach. But it doesn't stop there. There is one last thing.

Pay, Pay, Pay

In the year 2000, a movie came out of Hollywood that was an instant hit. It is the story of a young boy whose mother is an alcoholic and whose absentee father is abusive. In a social studies class, he is intrigued by his teacher's assignment—to think of something that could change the world and go do it. The young boy comes up with the idea of paying a favor forward instead of back. The concept is that when someone has done something for you, then pay it forward to someone else. The boy's actions created a revolution in other people's lives as they began to pay it forward, and the movie itself became the topic of much conversation on talk shows. It was as if this was a new concept that no one had ever heard of! The truth is that Jesus was the original "pay it forward" guy.

> *"Freely you received, freely give." (Matthew 10:8)*

Pay it forward. From beginning to end, Jesus taught us that we are to be channels of blessing, not reservoirs of blessing. When blessing flows into us, we are to let that blessing flow out to others.

How can you pay it forward? Not just by telling others where you found it, but by helping others when they want to discover it. This is where you get involved with others who want to change and you come alongside them to encourage and help them.

One of the things I have observed through the years about people who are in AA, NA, and other anonymous groups is their incredible willingness to help others who genuinely want help. It's a concept that is woven into the very fabric of the recovery process. If you have been given the gift of sobriety, then do whatever you can to help others receive the gift as well. They have freely received, and now they freely give.

In fact, anyone in recovery understands that their recovery will never be as strong as it could be until they begin to help others into the process. In other words, a person is not really walking in true recovery until they begin to carry the message to others.

In the very beginning of this process, I said that the goal is wholeness. Wholeness is the point in your growth and healing when you are able to give away more than you have to receive. In the early stages, sometimes all we can do is receive. In truth, we never come to the place where we no longer need to receive. We must always be receiving. But the goal of the process is to reach that place of maturity and growth where we are now able to give more than we have to receive. That's wholeness. That's emotional/spiritual maturity. That's our goal. That's when the blessings really begin to multiply in our own lives. When we give them away into others' lives.

In summary, the process and these principles can be boiled down to this.

ABC—Integrity. The beginning of blessing. Getting out of denial into truth.

DEFGHI—Perseverance. The addition of blessing. Getting into discovery. Cleaning up the messes we have made in our lives and the lives of others.

J—Wholeness. The multiplication of blessing. Carrying the message freely.

This is where blessing begins to grow exponentially in my life. When I begin to pay it forward. When I begin to give it away. That may mean I facilitate a group. It may mean I take someone on personally to mentor him or her in the process. It could mean that I just continue in a freedom group to be there to share my *help, hope,* and *healing* with others who are just beginning the process. However it happens, I want to give it away. Practice, Practice, Practice. Preach, Preach, Preach. Pay, Pay, Pay.

What are three ways that you can begin to pay, pay, pay, right now?

1. ______________________________

2. ______________________________

3. ______________________________

What is the most important thing you have learned in this step?

____

____

____

____

____

What do you intend to do this week as a result of this step?

____

____

____

____

TABLE TALK

What is the most important thing about you that relates to this chapter, that you are going to share with your spouse this week?

____

____

____

____

CONCLUSION

Well, there it is. You have completed the process! Or, have you? Not really. In reality, you have only started the process. You have begun the journey that needs to last a lifetime. Life change isn't just an event. It's a process. Now that you have the tools, you have the opportunity. The question is, "Do you have the tenacity?" Do you have the desire and the will? I pray that you do. So, now go . . . . Practice, Practice, Practice! Preach, Preach, Preach! Pay, Pay, Pay!

JOURNAL

Appendix 1: Guidelines for Facilitators

A CORE VALUE

An overall, core understanding for facilitators is that we are not counselors, teachers, or advisors. We are facilitators and guides of the process. Likewise, these are not counseling or advice groups. These are "one another" groups that utilize the tools God has given us for life change.

THE TOOLS ARE

1. A desire for change
2. One another
3. The Holy Spirit
4. Biblical principles of healing and change presented in the material
5. A caring and qualified facilitator

IMPORTANT FACILITATOR CHARACTERISTICS

1. Actively addressing your own issues
2. Open and willing to share in the group (lead with your weakness)

3. Willing to listen to members of the group

4. Able and willing to enforce the boundaries of the group

    a. Complete confidentiality of what is shared in the group
    b. No judging or condemning toward one another
    c. No cross-talk (allowing members of the group to talk to each other as another member is sharing)
    d. No fixing or advice giving allowed. When someone shares a problem or situation we do not give "advice" or try to "fix" the other person. We share from our own personal experience, strength, and hope and allow the Holy Spirit to lead the other person to make the application. If we have no personal experience, strength, or hope that relates to the issue, then we are to keep silent. When someone shares a problem or dilemma, the facilitator might ask, "Does anyone have any experience, strength or hope, to share that relates to that?"
        (1) Experience—Personal experience that relates, not hearsay or someone else's personal experience
        (2) Strength—How you have been strengthened to move through a similar situation (at least one that relates)
        (3) Hope—How you have found hope in the midst of something similar

5. Able to keep the group on task with the assigned material

6. Able to confront in a loving yet firm way when group boundaries are being crossed

7. Able to identify, train, and utilize an apprentice facilitator

Appendix 2: Suggested Discussion Questions

CHAPTER ONE: THE HEALING ENVIRONMENT

Opening the Session (10 minutes)

1. What was one of the happiest experiences of your childhood?
2. What is the need that brought you to this group?

Engaging the Process (10 minutes)

1. What are the three things the author says we must do as group members?
2. What did you write about your willingness to accept your role?
3. How does the author define "integrity"?
4. On a scale of 1 to 10 (10 is highest), how much integrity is in your life right now? Why is that?
5. Up to this point what has been your main fear about integrity in your life?
6. What does the "paradox of integrity" mean to you?

7. What is one thing you are going to need in order to persevere through the process?

8. How can this group help you to persevere?

9. When you read the author's definition of "wholeness" how did it make you feel?

10. What are some of the things you listed that you are the most grateful for?

Closing the Session (10 minutes)

1. What is one beneficial thing you have gotten out of this session?

2. What do you intend to share at "Table Talk" this week?

3. The next chapter is the Emotional/Spiritual Principle. Have you ever thought about how your emotional health connects to your spiritual health? In what way?

CHAPTER TWO: THE EMOTIONAL/SPIRITUAL PRINCIPLE

Opening the Session

1. What is one of happiest experiences of your adulthood?

2. How did Table Talk go this week?

Engaging the Process

1. What does the emotional/spiritual principle mean as stated by the author?

2. When you first read that principle, what did you feel or think?

3. What is the author's definition of spiritual maturity?

4. Based upon that definition, where would you put your spiritual maturity right now?

5. What struggles have you had in your intimacy with God?

6. What is the author's definition of emotional maturity?

7. Based upon that definition, where would you put your emotional maturity right now?

8. What are some things in your past that have affected your emotional maturity?

9. Can you see the biblical connection between the two? Explain that connection.

10. Can you think of some hurtful experiences that wounded you emotionally?

11. How have those wounds affected your relationships with others?

12. Referring to the emotional/spiritual, is there a place where you have been stuck? Can you understand why that has happened?

13. What do you think you need to do in order to move deeper into spiritual intimacy?

Closing the Session

1. What is one important thing you have learned this week?

2. What do you intend to share in Table Talk this week?

CHAPTER THREE: THE PILE PRINCIPLE

Opening the Session

1. In your home growing up who was responsible for taking out the garbage?

2. Why is taking out the garbage a task that no one enjoys?

3. How did Table Talk go this week?

Engaging the Process

1. In your own words, what does the Pile Principle mean?
2. What was the source of most of your pile (things said, done, or taken)?
3. What is one of the most hurtful things you have done to someone else?
4. What about your garbage do you think stinks the most to your spouse right now?
5. Where do you see your pile impacting your relationship with your spouse?
6. Up to this point where has your focus been? Your garbage? Your spouse's? Explain.
7. What are some things you need to do in order to deal with your pile?

Closing the Session

1. What is one really important thing you have learned in this chapter?
2. What is the thing you intend to share in Table Talk this week?
3. What relationships do you enjoy the most? Partnerships or competitions?
4. Next week's topic is partners or competitors. Which type of relationship do you and your spouse currently have?

CHAPTER FOUR: PARTNERS OR COMPETITORS?

Opening the Session

1. What is one meaningful partnership you have had in your life?
2. How did Table Talk go this week?

Engaging the Process

1. What are some differences between a partnership and a competition?

2. What are some expectations you brought into marriage?

3. Can you identify one expectation that might be unrealistic?

4. What is one expectation that you think your spouse brought into the marriage?

5. Did you enter marriage primarily to meet someone's needs or have yours met?

6. How would you describe how that view of needs has been working out for you?

7. What did you list as your spouse's top five needs?

8. How does that compare with Willard Harley's list?

9. What need of your spouse will you attempt to meet this week?

Closing the Session

1. What is one important truth you have learned in this chapter?

2. What do you intend to share at Table Talk this week?

CHAPTER FIVE: "A"—ADMIT POWERLESSNESS

Opening the Session

1. How did Table Talk go this week?

2. Has there ever been anything in your life that you had to admit you simply couldn't do? Explain.

Engaging the Process

1. How have you recognized any of the types of control (management) working in your life (image, God, people)?

2. Do you have a favorite tool you use to accomplish control?

3. What does the author mean by "effective" powerlessness?

4. What pain, if any, have you felt in your life from your attempts to control?

5. According to Einstein's definition of insanity, what evidence of insanity do you see in your life?

6. What are some red flags of warning you have recognized in your life?

7. What is one thing you are willing to admit powerlessness over in your marriage?

Closing the Session

1. What is one valuable thing you have learned in this session?

2. What do you intend to share this week at Table Talk?

CHAPTER SIX: "B"—BELIEVE THE TRUTH

Opening the Session

1. How did Table Talk go this week?

2. What was one myth you believed in childhood and later found out the truth? (Please, other than that there was no Santa Claus!)

3. How did you feel when you found out the truth?

Engaging the Process

1. In a sentence tell how you described what you believe about:

   - Yourself

   - Your spouse

   - Life

2. How open are you to discovering that what you said in the previous question

could be myth and not what you truly believe? (In other words, are you an honest doubter or dishonest doubter?)

3. What is one self-defeating behavior that you keep repeating in your life?

4. Do you agree or disagree with the principle that every behavior is based upon a belief? Explain.

5. How did you answer the question, "Is it possible to act contrary to what you believe?" What do you think about that?

6. Can you think of areas of your life where the "curse of knowledge" may be at work (i.e., an area where you have convinced yourself you believe something simply because you know it)?

7. Share one area where you see a contradiction between what you say you believe and your actual behavior. The behavior, belief, the lie.

8. Have you ever seen the "valley of despair" acted out in your life? How?

9. What do you need to do to change that lie into the truth?

Closing the Session

1. What is an important thing you have learned in this session?

2. What are you going to share with your spouse this week in Table Talk?

CHAPTER SEVEN: "C"—COMMIT TO CHRIST

Opening the Session

1. What is the greatest risk you have ever taken?

2. How did Table Talk go this week?

Engaging the Process

1. Using the opening story as a guide, what part of the story represents where you are right now in your spiritual life? In your marriage?

2. Which of the two forms of commitment to Christ have you made? Explain.
   - Partial
   - Complete
3. What difference has that commitment made in how you live your life?
4. What questions do you have about what complete commitment to Christ means?
5. What do you think is the difference between the "point" of surrender and the "process" of surrender?
6. How do you practice the "process" of surrender in your daily life?

Closing the Session

1. As a result of this chapter, what have you discovered that you need to do?
2. What is one important truth that you got from this chapter?
3. What do you intend to share this week at Table Talk?

CHAPTER EIGHT: "D"—DISCOVER RESPONSIBILITY

Opening the Session

1. Have you ever had someone blame you for something you had nothing to do with?
2. Have you ever blamed another person or a circumstance for something that you were really responsible for?
3. How did Table Talk go this week?

Engaging the Process

1. What do you feel when you think of engaging in this kind of rigorous honesty?

2. Can you see a connecting link between your life and your family of origin that needs to be broken?

3. What is the difference between a circumstance and a consequence?

4. What is a circumstance that you can identify in your life? What choices did you make as a result?

5. What is a consequence that you can identify in your life?

6. Given those definitions, is there anything in your life you have called a circumstance and now realize it could have been a consequence?

7. What is the difference between an explanation and an excuse?

8. In your marriage right now, what are you experiencing that is the result of choices (and thus are really consequences)?

9. Are you ready to be rigorously honest in your inventory?

Closing the Session

1. What is one important truth that you gained this week?

2. What are you going to share at Table Talk this week?

CHAPTER NINE: "E"—EXPOSE THE SECRETS

Opening the Session

1. When you were a kid, was there a friend that you told everything to?

2. How was that relationship different from your other friendships?

3. How did Table Talk go this week?

Engaging the Process

1. What experience did you have this past week as you began to work on your

inventory? (This inventory process will continue for weeks to come even as we move on to other chapters.)

2. In terms of the "propeller" illustration, is there any fishing line in your life that needs to be removed? What?

3. How have you experienced the truths that relationships thrive in the light of honesty and relationships die in the darkness of deception?

4. Do you have anything in your past you feel so guilty about that you can't imagine ever revealing it to anyone?

5. Using the hospital gown illustration, how open is your gown? Closed? Partially open? Half-open? Flapping in the breeze?

6. Do you have someone in mind that you can "Expose the Secrets" with?

Closing the Session

1. Can you imagine the freedom that would come in living life without secrets?

2. What is one important thing you learned about yourself this week?

3. What are you going to share this week at Table Talk?

CHAPTER TEN: "F" FOCUS ON FAITH

Opening the Session

1. What is one really risky thing you have done?

2. How did that make you feel after it was all over?

3. How did Table Talk go this week?

Engaging the Process

1. What character defects have you clearly identified in your life?

2. Pick one defect. What problems has that defect caused you in your life?

3. How ready (*listo*) are you to have your defects removed?

4. What is one defect that you are hesitant about giving up? Why is that?

5. What does the author mean by "faith is an action, not a thought"?

6. How does that relate to the premise and the promise? In other words, which comes first, the premise or the promise? Why is that true?

7. If you lived in the bizarro world, what are some things about you that would be different (the opposite of your character defects)?

8. What is the premise that you need to practice in one of those areas?

9. The author says, "Begin to talk to yourself and stop listening to yourself." What does that mean to you? How can you begin to do that?

Closing the Session

1. Up to this point in your life which have you done the most of—listening to yourself or talking to yourself?

2. What have you discovered about yourself this week?

3. What are you going to share this week at Table Talk?

CHAPTER ELEVEN: "G"—GO GET RIGHT

Opening the Session

1. What is one of your earliest memories of needing forgiveness and receiving it?

2. What did it feel like to be forgiven?

3. How did Table Talk go this week?

Engaging the Process

1. How ready are you to take full responsibility for harming others?

2. Explain why you do, or do not, feel ready to accept that responsibility.
3. Why does the Bible say we must first be willing to "give" forgiveness before we can ask for it from others?
4. Which of the three reasons for forgiving others—grace, guilt, or grief—means the most to you? Why is that?
5. Is there any place in your life where the "root of bitterness" has begun to grow?
6. Which one of the myths of forgiveness has hindered you from forgiving up till now?
7. Which part of the "What Forgiveness Is" discussion meant the most to you? Why is that?
8. Which one of the four points of "How Forgiveness Happens" encourages you the most?
9. Which one presents the greatest struggle for you?
10. What is it about making amends that causes you the most hesitation?
11. Is there anything you don't understand about the process of making amends?

Closing the Session

1. What are you going to do this week as a result of this chapter?
2. What are you going to share this week at Table Talk?

CHAPTER TWELVE: "H"—HEED THE WEEDS

Opening the Session

1. On a scale of 1 to 10, how good does your yard look during the growing season? Why is that true?

2. What would it require of you to improve the look of your yard?

3. How did Table Talk go this week?

Engaging the Process

1. What was your experience this week of beginning to forgive someone in your life?

2. How much progress did you make on your amends list this week?

3. Does your life look like your yard? How is your life different from your yard?

4. What is one area of your life where you have spent most of your time in the "circle of insanity"?

5. How has that been working out for you? What consequences have you seen from that?

6. What does it do in you when someone reacts rather than responds to you?

7. What are some situations in your life where you react rather than respond?

8. How can you imagine that doing a H.O.M.E. inventory could help in a specific situation? How about in your marriage?

9. Would you commit to doing the H.O.M.E. and E.D. every day for one week to see what difference it could make? Why or why not?

10. What are specific scenarios you know you will face this week that will challenge you to do a H.O.M.E. inventory?

Closing the Session

1. What is the most encouraging thing you have gained from this chapter?

2. What is the most challenging thing you have gained?

3. What do you intend to share at Table Talk this week?

CHAPTER THIRTEEN: "I"—INCREASE GOD CONTACT

Opening the Session

1. How did your H.O.M.E. and E.D. inventories go this week? Victories? Failures?

2. How did Table Talk go this week?

Engaging the Process

1. Do you feel that through the process thus far you have begun clearing out some of the hindrances to your intimacy with God?

2. How strong a grip do you have on the Word of God right now? Are you satisfied?

3. What do you need to do to increase that grip?

4. Up until now, which part of prayer have you focused on? The point of prayer or the process of prayer? Why is that?

5. What is the value of each one in your life?

6. What does your practice of confession before God look like right now (rarely, sometimes, daily, moment by moment through the day)?

7. Would you commit to an experiment of the three disciplines this week?

8. What is one step forward in each of the three disciplines that you will make and practice this week?

9. Share your answers with one another so you can get ideas from each other in the group.

Closing the Session

1. What encouraged you out of this session this week?

2. What will be your greatest challenge this week?

3. What are you going to share at Table Talk this week?

CHAPTER FOURTEEN: "J"—JUST DO IT!

Opening the Session

1. How did Table Talk go this week?

2. What experiences did you have with the "disciplines experiment" of the Word, prayer, and confession this week?

Engaging the Process

1. What has God shown you about yourself in this process so far?

2. What kinds of changes have you seen in your life as a result of practicing these principles?

3. Which part of the process has been the most beneficial to you (A through H)?

4. What do you have now that you can preach (your help, hope, and healing)?

5. How do you intend to do that from this point on?

6. Do you have anything you need to begin to "pay, pay, pay"? How can you do that?

7. What is one thing you intend to do immediately this week as a result of this step?

Closing the Session

1. What is the most important thing you have gained in this step?

2. What do you intend to share at Table Talk this week?

About the Author

As senior pastor of Fort Worth's City on a Hill, Dr. James Reeves regularly sees wounded people find hope and restoration through Jesus Christ.

After receiving his BA in Greek from Baylor University in 1976, James received his MDiv and DMin degrees from Southwestern Baptist Theological Seminary in 1981 and 1988.

He has been a pastor for more than thirty-five years. Since 1981 he has been a senior pastor. Since 1984 he has been the pastor of the same church, City on a Hill, which he came to soon after it was planted. Since 1992 that church has transitioned into the hospital church style of ministry.

James is no stranger to recovery circles. He was born into an alcoholic home and suffered the emotional wounds of a difficult childhood. In his mid-thirties, the bills began to come due in his life as the emotional wounds that he had glossed over and ignored for years started to surface. James nearly resigned from pastoral ministry but chose to confront his past and then used his newfound freedom in Christ to build a church based on resolving emotional woundedness issues for greater intimacy with God.

Today, in addition to his responsibilities at City on a Hill, known as "The Hospital Church," James speaks at seminars and mentors other churches seeking to make similar transitions to the hospital church model. James is willing to come to your place of ministry and equip you and your church to begin a help, hope, and healing ministry. At the time of this writing, James is able and willing to do this free of charge.

James's first book, *Refuge, How "Hospital Church" Ministry Can Change Your Church Forever,* was published by Kregel Publishers in the spring of 2010.

James and his wife, Laura, have two grown children. Tiffany, born in 1982, is a pediatric trauma nurse practitioner in a major children's hospital. Her husband is Davis. James and Laura's son, Zack, born in 1985, is a professional golfer. His beautiful wife is Ashley. James and Laura live near Fort Worth, Texas.